Being Truly
YOU

Discovering your own unique Wardrobe Personality
with Angela Marshall

for
WOMEN

Visit Angela Marshall's website:
www.appearancemanagement.co.uk
T. +44 (0)1372 388584

First published in the United Kingdom in 2008.

Matador Business
Troubador Publishing Ltd
9 De Montfort Mews, Leicester LE1 7FW, UK
Tel: +44 (0)116 255 9311
Fax: +44 (0)116 255 9323
e-mail: books@troubador.co.uk
www.troubador.co.uk/matadorbusiness

Graphic Design & Photography by Victoria Lee
Oktopuz Creative Services
www.oktopuz.co.uk

Illustrations by Chloe Webber
www.chloewebber.co.uk

Front/Back Cover Photographs by Victoria Lee:
Taken on location at Renaissance, 6 High Street, Reigate, Surrey, RH2 9AY, UK
Female model on back cover - Rebecca Hawkins

ISBN: 978-1906510-602
Printed in the UK by The Cromwell Press, Trowbridge, Wilts

Mixed Sources
Product group from well-managed
forests and other controlled sources
www.fsc.org Cert no. TT-COC-2082
© 1996 Forest Stewardship Council
FSC

Contents

Acknowledgements

This book has taken me two years in the writing as I have developed my information and researched my thoughts and ideas; it has only become reality with the help and support of many people. In acknowledgement, my gratitude goes to all who have given me their thoughts, feedback, suggestions and ideas. I cannot mention everyone, but I would like to express my thanks to you all.

Since this book is the result of my becoming an image consultant, and my experiences and the building of my knowledge over the years, I must take this opportunity, firstly to thank Veronica Croft at First Impressions, for training me (as an image consultant) and introducing me to the subject of Wardrobe Personality and secondly, my clients and friends, particularly those who have completed questionnaires and given me feedback on my ideas:

Carole Jackson, Mary Spillane and Barbara Jacques, with their books on image, which further increased my knowledge, particularly after I first trained; Victoria Lee, my graphic designer and Chloe Webber my illustrator, for helping me complete the book; Nikki, my friend, who trained as an image consultant and has always confirmed my beliefs on the subject and her two daughters Jenni and Lucy with their fresh, youthful ideas.

My final and most important acknowledgement must go to my husband, Stuart, who has encouraged and inspired me; without his support I would never have finished this book. I thank you all.

Angela

"Style is a reflection of your attitude and your personality."

SHAWN ASHMORE

Introduction

Do you know which clothes make you feel good as well as look good? How do you represent yourself to the world? Do your clothes reflect who you truly are? This book is about helping you to answer these questions and for you to understand your Wardrobe Personality. You will then have the confidence to dress to suit yourself and to be truly you. You will be able to adapt your wardrobe, achieve the most from your appearance and accomplish personal success through your own sense of style. A significant added benefit is that it should also save you money by helping you to avoid costly mistakes such as buying clothing from which you really won't get value for money.

Once you have understood your Wardrobe Personality you will be able to bring out the best in yourself and people will notice you for who you truly are. To answer the question – who is this book for? – ask yourself the following:

- **Do you want to own a wardrobe of clothes that you look and feel great in and look forward to wearing every day?**

- **Do you feel wonderful in some clothes, while in others you do not feel good at all, and want to understand why?**

- **Have you worn clothes that you have admired on others, but in which you feel uncomfortable and do not feel yourself?**

- Do you want to understand what styles of clothes you will enjoy wearing for various situations, such as for important business, school or social events?

- Do you care about how you come across to others through your appearance? Be honest, everyone likes compliments about the way they look!

- Do you want to show people how your appearance is a true reflection of you as a person – who you truly are?

- First impressions do count, so do you want people to recognise who you truly are, because the outer you represents the inner you?

- Do you want to benefit from understanding other Wardrobe Personalities and being able to adapt your approach accordingly?

Answer 'yes' to any or all of these and you will be much more aware how to acquire a wardrobe to suit the inner you after reading this book.

This book is for women, but I have written another for men. If you find this one interesting please do read the men's version, as it will help you understand and recognise the Wardrobe Personality of your husband, partner, brother, relative, friend or even business colleagues. It will help you to appreciate them for who they are, recognise why you may not always like what they wear and understand why they do, and why they may approach things differently to you. The latter point will enable you to anticipate how they will act at certain times (e.g. always up against deadlines, running late and disorganised, very dramatic, emotionally up and down, or meticulous in execution).

This book is neither prescriptive nor aimed at dictating what you should do or what you should wear, and you may not agree with everything I write. That's fine, but the underlying message is to encourage you to learn how to express your own style and to appreciate differences of opinion when it comes to appearance.

This is why people can turn up to the same event having interpreted one style quite differently to others.

Women have a vast choice when it comes to clothes. Which style? Which outfit combinations to mix and match? What is appropriate and comfortable to wear to work, to an event or just to walk the children to school? Women have so many more factors to take into account when choosing the correct clothes (far more than men). For example, when it comes to a formal event, a man need only to decide between a lounge or dinner suit, and then choose the shirt and tie. Whereas, a women should ask herself: "Can I wear trousers or does it need to be a skirt?... What length of skirt is appropriate – a cocktail dress or a full length evening gown?... Will it be cold do I need a jacket or a pashmina?... Which accessories will go with which neckline?... What underwear do I need to wear under the outfit tights, stockings and what shade should they be?... What accessories and what make-up, if any, shall I apply?"

When you do think you are wearing the right clothes, how do you feel? Do you feel great about yourself and do the clothes give you energy, lift your spirits and just make you feel wonderful? To look your best, yes, you need to be well-groomed, wear clothes that are a good fit, in the correct styles to enhance your body shape, and you should wear the right shades of colours to enhance your natural colouring. However, there may be times when you are not wearing the best shapes or colours, but still feel great or, conversely, you may be wearing the right shapes and colours, but not feel great at all! Why is this? Well, if the clothes do not represent your 'Wardrobe Personality' then you just won't feel right: you may feel overdressed, too casual, too trendy, too traditional or just too uncomfortable. Your clothes need to represent who you are, your inner you. Your Wardrobe Personality means more than the clothes in your wardrobe. The style of clothes you choose and the accessories you wear give out lots of messages about you and they need to represent who you truly are.

Being Truly You will help you understand your own particular Wardrobe Personality so that you will feel comfortable and, through the way you look, your clothes will represent your own unique personality. What you like will identify your Wardrobe Personality when you attend an event or go to work or even when you relax at home. Do you choose a pair of jeans, t-shirt and trainers rather than jogging bottoms, soft wool jumper and pumps to relax with the family or for an evening on your own watching TV? Our individual Wardrobe Personality is the most critical, but most overlooked factor when we consider how we might improve our appearance and develop our personal image and personal brand.

So many magazines, books and television programmes completely ignore our own individual personalities and try to shoehorn us into wearing the latest fashion, when we may well have no interest in up-to-the-minute trends and prefer either comfort, a more traditional look or even to create our own bizarre style. Many books have been written over the years on personal image and branding and TV listings are full of 'experts' advising celebrities or members of the public how they should present themselves. However, my book is designed to help you understand how to dress to represent the inner you and to show the world who you really are. This means finding your Wardrobe Personality; a subject that is so often overlooked and yet which is, to me, the most important aspect of managing your individual appearance.

Disclosing the inner you

Body shape and colouring, personal image and branding are very important, but the key is first to understand your own Wardrobe Personality so that it can shine through. Your Wardrobe Personality is a reflection of your own distinctive character, of the inner you. Once you have discovered your Wardrobe Personality, you can build and develop your own unique style, for whatever occasion; you will be yourself and not what others think you should be. Then, combined with the knowledge of which shades of colours and shapes of clothes best suit your body, you will present yourself at your very best.

This book will enable you to discover your Wardrobe Personality. To assist, I have identified the 10 most common Wardrobe Personalities by recognising that we now live in a much more varied society than years ago, with much greater influences on fashion and our life styles. We travel more, we may be mothers with full-time careers; changing nappies one minute and running an office the next. All this affects how we wish to dress. However, it is the combination of the various Wardrobe Personalities and how we define different roles through our clothes that makes us unique. Find out which one(s) you are: most people will be a combination of at least two Wardrobe Personalities with a stronger primary and then other influential secondary ones. Often one will be more appropriate for the working environment or for a mum and housewife at home, whilst the other will be more evident in your personal or social life.

The purpose of this book is to help you recognise the origins of your style and why you interpret fashion differently to others. When you know your Wardrobe Personality it will help you understand why you may have a fetish for clothes, shoes and bags and/or follow the latest trends or, on the contrary, have no real interest in clothes. You will understand why certain clothes, fabrics, textures, patterns and accessories make you feel on top of the world while others make you feel uncomfortable, garish or dreary. You may have received a colour analysis and discovered there are some shades in your palette which you don't like or would never wear. Maybe during a style consultation you have been recommended a few styles that, again, you would never dream of being seen in. This is due to the fact that, whilst they may be appropriate for you, they are simply not suited to your Wardrobe Personality.

People wear different styles of clothes to the same event or to work. For example just think of how the female television news presenters vary with their different clothes, accessories and make-up. Take Moira Stuart, Sophie Raworth, Kate Silverton and Natasha Kaplinsky; they all have styles that reflect their personalities. Wouldn't it be boring if we were all the same?

As I have mentioned, this book does not dictate what you should and should not wear. It will help you to adapt your own style for different life situations and I hope it will give you the knowledge to wear your individual style with confidence and stay true to your most valuable asset – your personality.

Recognise the Wardrobe Personality of your friends and family
A further benefit of this book is that by understanding your own Wardrobe Personality you will start to recognise the Wardrobe Personality of your friends, family and work colleagues. You will begin to understand which Wardrobe Personalities you are most likely to get on with and the strengths and differences

of each. For instance, Fashion Fads (p.90) generally pay a great deal of attention to the latest fashion and, consequently, will constantly shop to buy the latest clothes, spending time getting ready to go out, whereas a Casual (p.62) will have no interest in fashion and will only shop for items when needed, spending little time getting ready to go out. Often the Fashion Fad will enjoy face to face socialising, going to the latest clubs and partying, whilst the Casual may well favour a quieter lifestyle drinking with friends in the pub, or prefer using social networking websites to face-to-face networking. Knowing the Wardrobe Personality of others will be hugely helpful when we go into longer term relationships, either professionally or personally. This is covered in more detail in Chapter 7.

So, whatever your age, size, colouring or race, please do not live your life wearing the clothes others want you to wear, or what you think you should wear to please others. Wear clothes that make you feel great as well as look great, and that show the inner you. Be proud of yourself, show the world the inner you, be different, and be truly you.

Angela Marshall

• • • • •

"Good clothes open all doors."

THOMAS FULLER

CHAPTER ONE

My Discovery of Wardrobe Personality

In 1995, I trained as an Image Consultant and learned about the various Wardrobe Personalities (although at that time I worked with only five variations). No sooner had I learnt about the subject than I immediately recognised the benefits of understanding my own Wardrobe Personality. It helped me to appreciate why I was not comfortable in some clothes and yet loved others. It also gave me the confidence to create my own style and to dress in what pleases me, not what other people like, and to project my true personality without being inappropriately dressed for location or occasion. I recognised that we all have different personalities, our inner selves, and that this is reflected in what we like to wear.

I also understood why I felt great dressed in smart tailored clothes, but struggled to look and feel good in relaxed or informal clothes at weekends. I understood why I wanted to take more clothes on holiday than some of my friends and why it took me longer to pack. I often wanted to take more shoes, a choice of make-up plus a couple of handbags, whilst one of my friends preferred to pack lots of sports gear, only two pairs of shoes, little make-up, if any, and only the bag she travelled with.

Feeling good and looking good

I recognised why I did not feel good in clothes that I liked on other people, not necessarily because the shapes or colours were wrong, but because the fabric, style and/or detail did not suit my Wardrobe Personality. I acknowledged that compared to one friend, I liked softer jersey cotton to stiff cotton and that it was important for me to wear clothes made of quality fabrics but with a slightly contemporary feel. I knew I was not comfortable in 'cheap and cheerful' fabrics with big fancy detail, whereas she loved stiff cotton shirts and preferred to spend her money on cheap clothes and have spare money for going to various sports activities. I also looked at clothes in magazines and liked them, but recognised that if I actually wore them myself I would feel uncomfortable as they would not feel right if they were too loose, fancy or outlandish for me.

I understood why my Mum didn't wear make-up every day – when she did it was only powder and lipstick – whereas I felt uncomfortable without my full make-up unless relaxing at home or on holiday. I understood why my sister liked fancy handbags and always spent time on her hair so that it always looked right. Why she has lots of cushions, ornaments and pictures in her home and likes a quaint cottage and fewer modern items compared to me. When I was at school and my father took me shopping, I knew that while I appreciated the high quality clothes he bought for me, I often wanted something a bit more fashionable. I did not always like what he wanted me to have and I certainly did not like his choice of shoes! He went for plain and practical – well, he was a farmer – whereas I wanted fashionable high heels with some detail. His Wardrobe Personality was not quite the same as mine. This applies to this day.

Once I understood my Wardrobe Personality, I no longer bought clothes I would not feel happy in. On the odd occasion when I did make a mistake, I would get them home, realise I didn't feel good in them as they were not my personality, and decide to take them back and learn from the experience. I have learned what to avoid and what to look for to suit my Wardrobe Personality. Linen, for instance, is very stylish for the summer these days, but if I bought clothes in this fabric in the past I never liked them. I do not enjoy wearing clothes that crease and I do not like the fabric's starchy feel. However, a linen mix is ideal for me when I dress casually, as I don't mind some creases in a more relaxed style. However, I always have to press the items after a few outings!

Attracted to people with similar Wardrobe Personalities

I noticed that my husband and close friends all have at least one Wardrobe Personality that is the same as mine; this is, I believe, why we get on so well.

I have also noticed that happy couples nearly always have one Wardrobe Personality in common.

My husband, Stuart, and I are people who like to be tidy. We like a mix of some traditional and some contemporary items and we have our own sense of style. We like quality items with a contemporary look, but are not interested in wearing the latest trend. We both like a variety of accessories to express our personalities and complete our style. However, Stuart likes natural crisp materials such as cotton and denim, plain with no fussy detail, whereas I like materials with softness, such as cashmere or jersey or some synthetic fabrics, such as Lycra, with a little fancy detail. He certainly has as many shoes as me, although we often criticise each other's styles of shoes; this is often due more to our differing body shapes including our feet. Even our choice of shower gel is quite different; Stuart likes a zingy feel while I like something silky smooth. This is nothing to do with male versus female: female friends with a similar Wardrobe Personality to Stuart like similar brands to him. (Understanding this could help manufacturers to market their brands in a more targeted and effective way.)

Appreciate one another's tastes

Stuart and I have grown to appreciate and understand our different ideas and tastes. We have learned to adapt, particularly with joint projects, so that we can both be happy. For instance, in the home I like to change things on a more regular basis and I prefer more colour in rooms and fancy details on furniture and home accessories. So, to satisfy both our personalities, we have agreed to keep the decoration of the walls in the house plain, but we have bought paintings we both like and added colourful cushions, ornaments and candles that provide contrast and which I can move around or replace. In practice, this means recognising that our personalities are not exactly the same.

As a Gamin (p.70) Stuart looks immaculate all the time, without much effort; whether dressed in a suit on a very hot day, travelling to and from the City of London, or when he has thrown on a pair of jeans and a t-shirt for working around the house, he always looks great. He is also likely to have more or less the same physique all his life due to his small and neat frame. In contrast, I don't have a Gamine build and in the past I struggled to look neat and felt out-of-sorts in informal or casual clothes, especially on a hot summer's day, when I compared myself to Stuart. Now that I know what styles and fabrics I like on me and feel comfortable in a casual look that works for me, I am much happier in my casual wear. It works for my Wardrobe Personality and buxom build!

I now understand why Stuart tends to go into great detail about things and why he takes longer than me to make up his mind when he is buying clothes, choosing holidays or deciding on home improvements. I tend to look at the bigger picture and decide quickly. He is meticulous with detail in areas that are important to him, but less organised with other things. I am not so meticulous, but always like being organised and will use the help of other people to make things perfect when necessary.

I am truly comfortable showing off my Wardrobe Personality. I understand and accept that it is okay to be different to my friends and family and that I can look and feel great, by being me. I always like to wear what is appropriate to various events, but in my own style and Wardrobe Personality.

Value other Wardrobe Personalities

My experience has also helped me to understand and value other Wardrobe Personalities: by knowing what their interests and styles are likely to be from the way they dress. I am less critical of other people's styles as I appreciate and recognise they have different approaches and interests. For example, people who are more creative, fashion-conscious, sporty or traditional will dress differently. People are often surprised at how much I can tell about them from the way they put their clothes together, especially from the style of shoes they wear. I can often guess their hobbies and interests and, even if we are discussing their wardrobe over the telephone, I can guess their preference in styles and fabrics and what accessories and make-up, if any, they may like.

Understand how to feel happy in your clothes

What I do hope this book will do is help you to fully understand yourself and to help you be 'truly you', so that you will feel happy, confident and at ease in your clothes. On rare occasions when you do not, you will recognise the reasons why and learn from them. Life is not perfect and neither are we!

I also hope you will appreciate why people dress differently to you. The world would be very uninteresting if we were all the same and went about things in the same way. Appreciate others for who they are and recognise their strengths – like you and me, they are unique and special.

• • • • •

"Elegance is a question of personality, more than one's clothing."

JEAN–PAUL GAULTIER

CHAPTER TWO

The Clothes You Choose to Wear Convey Significant Messages

Some people spend all their time worrying about what to wear to an event and whether or not people will like what they wear. They have no confidence and do not recognise that they may have a different Wardrobe Personality to someone else and that they will therefore have different opinions and ideas to them. Other people have said to me that they are not interested in how they look as it is more important who they are as a person. However, I think deep down everyone cares, as we all enjoy compliments on how we look and, if you do not care about yourself, then why should anybody else?

Some of my clients may have said they don't care about their appearance, but then decided to do something about it (because they have received a gift or been advised by their employers to improve their appearance). It is surprising how often after a consultation and/or shopping trip their body language changes in a constructive way and their self-esteem just grows. They not only look, but feel good.

Let me give you a couple of examples:

A client came to me, on the advice of her company. She was a supervisor, very good at her work, but lacking in confidence with clients and her appearance let her down. She was a large lady and wore baggy clothes in plain colours with no accessories or make-up. She thought the clothes would hide her size, felt bad in them and consequently had lost interest in clothes. After a consultation, which included discussing her Wardrobe Personality, she understood how she could bring out her romantic, bubbly personality. We went on a shopping trip and, by choosing the styles and fabrics of clothes, together with various accessories, we brought out her flamboyant Wardrobe Personality and she started to enjoy her wardrobe. She received lots of compliments which meant she was regularly smiling and laughing – her self-esteem increased. She looked smarter and was surprised by how her colleagues and clients almost immediately treated her differently. She began to enjoy shopping and knew what to look for (including wearing lots of colour, make-up and a variety of jewellery. She found her true self.

On another occasion, an IT consultant who had set up her own business and had previously worked for an airline, met me at a networking event. After finding out what I did she said she had not taken an interest in her appearance whilst an employee, but now she was self-employed she had decided she wanted to look better. After a consultation, she was amazed, not only at how great she felt, but also at her confidence when speaking to people she previously would not have. She also realised why she had been overlooked for promotion in her previous job. She was amazed how her friends complimented her and noticed how much more energetic and positive she was to life. She recognised the style of clothes that made her feel and look good and that she needn't worry about fancy clothes, details and high heels for work. They were not her Wardrobe Personality.

What are these messages?

Most people will be familiar with the phrase 'never judge a book by its cover' but, to be honest, we still do. What you wear and the way you put your look together, including your hairstyle and accessories, send out numerous messages about you. Usually, within the first 3-5 seconds of meeting, people will subconsciously decide whether or not they like and/or trust you, or want to do business with you (either socially or commercially). Now, I know a lot of us can talk fast, but 3-5 seconds is not much time in which impress, is it? So this initial view can only have been reached on the basis of what they have seen; essentially how you look, or appear and how you behave.

The clothes you wear and how you wear them are giving out lots of messages about you as an individual. It is not necessarily a case of right versus wrong, although it can be a case of appropriate or inappropriate. Your clothes are an indication or representation of what you are like as a person and they play an important part in how you come across to others. Your style will also indicate whether you are trendy, classic, creative, dramatic, conservative, sporty or casual, even whether you are tidy or untidy, or pay a great deal of attention to detail. What you are showing to the outside world is an indication of what you are like on the inside.

Looking stylish comes more easily to some than others. Some people have a natural talent for it whilst others have to work a little harder and need more help. After reading this book you will be able to identify your own personal preferences of clothes, styles and materials. You will recognise why you feel comfortable or uncomfortable wearing different materials (say linen versus jersey cotton, natural denim to Lycra in denim or a chino, fine wool to knobbly wool) and why you prefer a particular shoe or other accessory.

True representation

Understanding your Wardrobe Personality may even help you to find the right person for a new relationship. If you are a tidy-minded person, could you cope with living with someone who left their belongings all over the place? You might prefer to spend your money on a modern abstract painting, but what if your partner longs to have exquisite antiques adorning the shelves or spend the money on a fabulous holiday? When we know and understand our Wardrobe Personality and those of others, it can influence our life choices.

You may also be able to understand how you can identify the type of house, furnishings and even the friends, colleagues or jobs that you will most likely be drawn to.

A client, Sara, who I would describe as a Romantic Casual - (you will learn about this later, but essentially they like things colourful, feminine, relaxed, but in a casual style) worked for a law firm in London dealing with Mergers & Acquisitions departments of banks. She dressed, generally, in colourful tops and fashionable jewellery, but in a very informal, casual style. She frequently didn't wear make up and her hair was long and untidy. Sara was advised, by her boss, that it would be advisable to smarten up her appearance and to wear clothes that looked more professional. After a few months she noticed there was a position available in the Media section dealing with film producers and radio stations. Sara applied for the job and got it. She found that she was much happier and that her appearance fitted in much better with her new colleagues and clientele.

Sara's experience

Sara, having had a consultation on Wardrobe Personality, recognised that her Wardrobe Personality and personal image clashed with that of her work department; that she would find it hard to look very neat all the time, as it wasn't her nature and that she would feel uncomfortable in traditional classic style clothes. She recognised that the media industry was more in line with her own Wardrobe Personality; this helped her career and she felt much more comfortable with people of similar Wardrobe Personality. Understanding this can gain you insight into your own character and that of others. In turn, this can help you when you are faced with important decisions. You can avoid making all sorts of mistakes, both professionally and personally.

Mix and match for best results

Often we will have one look for work and a completely different look for our personal life. Why? Well, most people are a combination of one or two Wardrobe Personalities. We are likely to have at least one dominant, or primary Wardrobe Personality complemented by a secondary characteristic. By the successful marrying of our personalities, we have the freedom to mix and match to achieve the best result. We may even have a combination of three Wardrobe Personalities, particularly I have noticed, if it involves a Dramatic Wardrobe Personality. More of this in Chapter 6.

Once you understand your Wardrobe Personality you will feel confident about creating an exclusive style with which you feel comfortable. You will not fall in with what others like or what magazines, or the media, tell you to wear. Wardrobe Personality helps you to understand the type of person you are. It also enables you to give out the messages you want to convey and to more accurately recognise the true characteristics of others.

Is your wardrobe a true reflection of your Wardrobe Personality?

More often than not, people have wardrobes full with clothes that they hardly ever wear. The old 80/20 rules applies: 80% of the time they wear only 20% of their clothes. Does this sound familiar? If so, what's your excuse? Possibly, you have bought on impulse, not sorted out your wardrobe in a long while and still have clothes that you wore many years ago. It could be that you rarely wear some clothes because you do not feel great in them or because other people, such as your partner, daughter, friend, sister or even the shop assistant, persuaded you to buy them. Alternatively you may have chosen the clothes in a hurry, because they were in fashion or perhaps you bought them in the sales because they were cheaper. It's quite likely that you don't wear these clothes, as they do not really match your Wardrobe Personality.

Recognising and understanding our Wardrobe Personality is one of the most critical aspects in determining what we should wear. Some of us enjoy dressing up and looking highly polished, yet others may find this a complete pain and prefer a more relaxed look with looser, less fitted styles.

It is important that we wear clothes that truly reflect our personality and we should adapt accordingly but also appropriately for the circumstances.

Looking for a job promotion

If you are looking for promotion you should ask yourself whether or not you dress appropriately for the position. It may be that you have become complacent with your style, so you should look to refresh your approach by considering how you should present yourself, whilst at the same time bringing out your true Wardrobe Personality. When you do this, you will find that you look good, feel good and, by playing to your strengths, you will be more positive. People will then react to you more positively. If your style is at complete odds to the company, then it may be that you would not fit in with the culture of the people anyway!

After having a baby

You may have had your first baby and, having worked in a very formal environment, you find you need different clothes now that you are at home with your newborn. Other mothers you meet may be very trendy, but this may not be your style. Buying different clothes for a new lifestyle still needs to reflect your Wardrobe Personality, which may well be different to both the business look you once enjoyed and some of the people you meet in your new environment. Learn to understand what works for you. After completing the questionnaire in Chapter 4 you will understand what you will feel good in.

Becoming more adventurous

You may on occasions want to be a little dramatic or creative, while at other times be more sporty or casual. You can do this with simple changes, such as adapting your hairstyle with hair products and/or changing the style of a blouse or shoes, wearing some make-up or stronger colours to give you a different look for the occasion. At the end of the day, however, you should always feel 'truly you'.

What determines our Wardrobe Personality?

Many different aspects go into making up a Wardrobe Personality, but it is most clearly represented in the styles of clothing, fabrics, accessories and whether we wear make-up or no make-up. The huge variety of fabrics and textures on the market today contribute more to our style than you might realise. We have, to name but a few, linen, cotton, wool, tweed, corduroy, denim, jersey, cashmere, chiffon, silk, viscose, acrylic and a variety of other new manmade fabrics. Do they crease? Are they soft-feel fabrics or stiff? Are they fine, knobbly or bulky materials? What accessories do we like? Are they large, small, bold, modern, classic, high quality, cheap, fancy or simple or do we prefer none at all? It is important that we appreciate how much our choice influences the image we project to other people. When we feel comfortable in our clothes we look and act confidently, and this includes our body language.

Your shoes and their message

One of the easiest ways to identify a person's Wardrobe Personality is by looking at their shoes. Shoes give out lots of messages depending on the style, colour, how clean they are and what condition they are in. When buying shoes we make decisions based on whether we like the colour or style, seek comfort, wish to make a fashion statement, or look elegant or smart, and whether they are for business, sport or social occasions. Do you ever look at someone else's accessories, such as their watch, jewellery or shoes, and think: I don't like them, I could never buy or wear them, or do you think, I love them? Whether you wear shoes for a special event or just to go walking, you will only wear them if you like them. (Even if you have medical problems such as back or knee problems you will try to choose what is the nearest to your Wardrobe Personality.) All of these choices send out strong messages about your Wardrobe Personality.

Your styles give out information about yourself

The look you choose, from the styles, the fabrics to the accessories, gives out lots of information about yourself.

Let me give you a couple of examples:

> **HR Managers**
>
> Two colleagues work for a large corporate consultancy firm; both regard themselves as smart, but they have very different images. The first likes a black skirt and checked jacket, fitted very neatly to her figure. She wears a white top, simple silver necklace and earrings, and highly polished court shoes. Her hair is neat and short and she always wears simple make-up.
>
> The second likes black trousers, a red top with a loose fitted bell sleeved cardigan with concealed popper fastenings. She likes flat, plain pump shoes in black, often needing a polish, no jewellery, and her unkempt, long frizzy hair and her make-up (consisting of lip-gloss and mascara) is only worn on days of important meetings.
>
> The first woman likes to look smart in a simple neat style; she will be organised in planning her work, worrying about the small detail. She is fairly conservative and doesn't like too much change. The second woman prefers a relaxed style;

she will be less organised and will underestimate the time available, but not worry so much about small details and can see the bigger picture.

These women interpret "smart professional" in a different way because of the differences in their Wardrobe Personality.

Hairdressers

Two women who work as hairdressers are both dressed in black, but their styles of clothes and shoes are very different. One is very petite in a simple denim mini skirt and t-shirt; she wears comfortable plain black pumps, has no make-up and a short, neat bobbed hairstyle. The other wears a puffball skirt with fancy detail on the waistline and a frill sleeved top, red button kitten heel shoes and has long flowing, wavy hair. Both are giving out different messages as they have different Wardrobe Personalities. As you will discover later, the first woman is a Gamine Wardrobe Personality who likes to be neat and organised with no fuss. She likes every detail to be correct and feels good in simple comfortable clothes that look neat and fit well. The second woman reflects a Romantic Wardrobe Personality. She likes to feel feminine, always wears make-up, enjoys wearing accessories and likes to be expressive and imaginative.

• • • • •

"We are shaped and fashioned by what we love."

JOHANN WOLFGANG VON GOETHE

CHAPTER THREE

The Advantages of Understanding Your Wardrobe Personality

Recognising your Wardrobe Personality will not only help you to understand how to get the most use out of your wardrobe, by appreciating your own sense of style and which fabrics, styles and accessories create it, but also help you to enjoy and feel good in your clothes. This will increase your self esteem and you will have the confidence to be able to adapt your appearance to suit various occasions. Once you have understood your Wardrobe Personality you will be able to bring out the best in yourself and people will notice you for who you truly are. Also, it will help you to learn more about the Wardrobe Personality of others.

One of the advantages of this is that you will ultimately save yourself a lot of money. Why? Because you will only buy new items that match your Wardrobe Personality. This means no more items stuck at the back of the wardrobe unloved and unworn. Also, you will gain greater value from the clothes you do purchase by considering the 'cost per wear'. If you buy an item for £50 and only wear it twice, its cost per wear is £25, whereas if you buy an item for £300 but wear it 30 times, its cost per wear is only £10.

Adapting and changing as you change

Understanding your Wardrobe Personality will help you to choose clothing that really does suit you, and it will help prevent you buying garments purely to please other people like your friends, family or colleagues. They may have different Wardrobe Personalities to you and will be recommending what they like! However, you will obviously need to recognise how to adapt your style to fit in with certain events and with your corporate/working environment. From a dress perspective, the working environment has become an interesting place in recent years with more general acceptance of dress-down, or casual days. Just think how people in your workplace interpret 'casual day' differently. How we interpret what is appropriate will provide a strong insight into our Wardrobe Personality. As your lifestyle changes, so you may want to adapt your Wardrobe Personality. You will have a core Wardrobe Personality, particularly for your time at home relaxing, but do allow your Wardrobe Personality to develop as you change and use this book as a reference. I know I have adapted and changed since leaving my first career (in banking) and becoming an image consultant. Although my core Wardrobe Personality is still very similar, I know how to update and change it to suit my age and lifestyle.

> For example, say you are a yoga teacher and you go to a networking group which has mostly accountants, lawyers, estate agents and bankers who are mostly suited and booted. You may find they will relate to you better if you wear a jacket (in a style and fabric to suit your relaxed and entrepreneurial business style) with trousers or a skirt and heels. On the other hand, if you meet up with a group of young mums, you may wish to dress in jeans and a top with trainers. All of these are in the styles to suit your Wardrobe Personality and yet they are appropriate for the occasion.

So you adapt your dress style and approach to suit the circumstances, but you still need to stay true to your own style and personal brand. This is how you use your Wardrobe Personality.

How Wardrobe Personality influences everything we do

With an understanding of your Wardrobe Personality you will recognise what accessories, styles and fabrics of clothing you feel comfortable in and it will give you greater confidence because you will feel comfortable and more confident. You will wear styles that make you happy and are a reflection of who you really are. You will understand why you feel great in some clothes and accessories, but not in others. You will recognise why some clothes you have worn in the past made you feel overdressed, self-conscious, dowdy, out-of-date or too trendy, even when others said you looked good. You will recognise why you do not like things that other people think are great and understand why they like them. Get it wrong and you can feel self-conscious; get it right and you feel wonderful and it is one less thing to worry about.

One of my clients worked in the sales department of a pharmaceutical company which was very traditional in both approach and dress. However, she preferred to have a more casual image and create new ideas, but found that her colleagues related to things differently to her. She also found her ideas did not fit in with her colleagues and bosses, so she eventually applied to work for a different company. She found the new company had a completely different approach to their work: they were open to new ideas, had a more relaxed style and her new colleagues' image was more in tune with her own. Not only was she much happier, but also she actually progressed through the firm much more quickly than she would have done by staying where she was.

Benefits in summary:

Once you understand and recognise your Wardrobe Personality you will:

- Know what styles of clothes, fabrics, textures, patterns and accessories you are comfortable in and enjoy wearing and, conversely, what to avoid;

- Understand why you feel uncomfortable when you make the odd error and learn from the mistake;

- Know how to express yourself in a way that still keeps you feeling comfortable and confident – whatever the mood or event;

- Not follow the crowd, but have your own unique style;

- Be able to identify other Wardrobe Personality types and understand how better to approach and communicate with them; (this can help in both social and business situations.)

- Understand what type of brands, homewares and products you will enjoy and why;

- Understand why a friend or partner likes different items to you and learn how to adapt to one another;

- Avoid the mistakes of buying what you like in magazines or see on others, or what the shop assistant, friends or family suggest, but which do not fit in with your Wardrobe Personality.

Creating the right image

Understanding your Wardrobe Personality will help you to bring out your personal image both in business and in your social life. It will also help you to express your own personal brand. When you have the right hairstyle and are dressed in a style of clothes and accessories that reflects you, people will instantly recognise you for who you truly are.

Looking good, feeling good with a great wardrobe of clothes

When you know what you like, you will enjoy your clothes and be happy with your look. When you understand and know what items to buy, you will be able to mix and match garments much more easily and you will find you need fewer clothes for your lifestyle. However, certain Wardrobe Personalities will always have more clothes than others and they will like to change them more frequently. When you know your own style and the type of textures and fabrics you prefer, you will then feel in control, more comfortable and more confident with your appearance. This, in turn, will increase your self-esteem. You will behave in a more positive way and people like being with positive people. Some Wardrobe Personalities do not like trying new things, but even they will find it easier to experiment and will look and feel good knowing they are wearing a style that compliments their inner self.

Discover your Wardrobe Personality

Before I describe each of the Wardrobe Personalities in detail you should complete the questionnaire in the next chapter to discover your own Wardrobe Personality. It is important to complete the questionnaire first, otherwise you may make the mistake of searching for the Wardrobe Personality you would like to be in the various questions; this would obviously skew the results. You are what you are, so there's no point in pretending! You may even find it useful for a close friend or relative to complete the questionnaire for you and then to compare the results to yours. Why? Well we do not always see ourselves as others do!

Through my business I have helped many clients bring out their Wardrobe Personality. After a consultation, they recognise how they can change and adapt their appearance and learn how to feel great in what they should wear. Now they are wearing the style of clothes, fabrics and accessories that suit them; they feel more confident, start to achieve things they never dreamed of and discover that people react to them more positively, both socially and in business. They also find they attract people of similar interests.

Our Wardrobe Personality is an expression of our own personality; our inner self. We generally have a core, primary Wardrobe Personality that will remain with us throughout our lives, but it may evolve as we ourselves alter and develop.

• • • • •

"Luxury must be comfortable, otherwise it is not luxury."

COCO CHANEL

CHAPTER FOUR

The Questionnaire - Discovering Your Wardrobe Personality

It's time to complete the questionnaire and see what Wardrobe Personality you are. Read the following questions and tick the answer that most closely reflects your views.

Answer all the questions as quickly as possible – first responses are normally the most accurate.

You may even find it useful for a close friend or relative to complete the questionnaire for you and then to compare the results to yours. Why? Well we do not always see ourselves as others do.

1. Which of the following best sums up your approach to clothes?

❏ **A.** I am not interested in fashion, but prefer to think of comfort and what is practical. I prefer relaxed, loose-fit styles, nothing too fitted or fancy. I prefer inexpensive clothes with an informal look.

❏ **B.** I like casual styles that have ease of movement and are easy to wash and wear. I like layers that can easily be added or taken off, which are easy to pack; I prefer informal clothes, but with a sporty look.

❏ **C.** I like clothes that fit well and are comfortable and simple. I like to look neat whether for formal or informal occasions, according to my lifestyle.

❏ **D.** I like well-fitted clothes that are timeless: good value for money, simple designs with a co-ordinated structured look. I find a formal look easier than a casual one.

❏ **E.** I like high quality contemporary, classic styles that look elegant – nothing too harsh or too body hugging - that suit my shape and fit well. I like to have a stylish look that is always appropriate for the occasion.

❏ **F.** I like bold styles with unusual proportions that make a statement, yet look sophisticated and stylish: nothing conventional or predictable.

❏ **G.** I like to look and feel feminine with flowing softer cuts and fancy detail and I enjoy colour. I will give attention to detail to achieve the complete look, from the colour of my tights to my jewellery.

❏ **H.** I like clothes that are the latest fashion that will show I am up-to-the-minute in style.

❏ **I.** I aim to look pretty, gentle and feminine and will take time to look good. I like neat fitted styles that are sexy and colourful and will spend whatever time it takes to look right.

❏ **J.** I like an original look with unusual styles that are my own creation. I like to adapt my clothes in an unpredictable way that gives an artistic or hippy style. I like a variety of colours and combinations of fabrics.

2. Which of the following statements about shoes most reflects what you would choose?

(styles will be according to your lifestyle)

❑ **A.** I go for comfortable, practical, unfussy styles and only have a few pairs, nothing extravagant; I prefer flat heels, only wearing a small heel for special occasions (e.g. leather loafers, velcro fastening trainers, crocs, chunky sole boots).

❑ **B.** I have several pairs of trainers of known brands, flat boots and I wear heels for smart occasions (e.g. brand trainers, loafers, flat riding boots or high knee boots).

❑ **C.** I like a few neat, simple shoes for my lifestyle: nothing fancy or colourful (e.g. trainers, plain black or brown pumps with two straps, leather brogues, flat pixie or fitted leather calf boots).

❑ **D.** I like good quality, good value, simple plain styles that are timeless in neutral colours for work, casual wear and walking (e.g. plain court shoes, 2" heel plain ankle or pull on knee length boots).

❑ **E.** I like contemporary classic styles that give an elegant look. I like to keep them in peak condition and they must be high quality (e.g. patent ballerina, tan leather buckle boots, crocodile skin court shoes).

❑ **F.** I like highly polished shoes that are exaggerated in style or in colour and make a statement (e.g. very high or pointy stilettos, thigh boots).

❑ **G.** I love my shoes from formal to casual to evening styles, from wedges, kitten heel, peep toe to high stiletto in colours or with some details (e.g. lace-up boots, black patent stilettos with ankle strap, coloured pumps with bows, knee high heel boots with buckles).

❑ **H.** I like styles, colours and brands from this season's trends and have several pairs for various events (e.g. Ugg boots, platform 3–4" heel pumps, patent platform or wedge boots).

❑ **I.** I like neat pretty shoes in meticulous condition, preferably high or with fancy sequins, a pattern or bows (e.g. trainers with sequins, kitten pink shoes, sling backs with crossover sequin details, pink pumps with polka dot bows).

❑ **J.** I like bizarre shoes in unusual styles or colours (e.g. biker boots, heavy lace up boots, metallic wedge, peep toe, high red stilettos, nothing classic or plain).

3. What is your wardrobe like?

☐   **A.**   Untidy, mix match on wire hangers all mixed up; shoes scattered everywhere, rarely sorted.

☐   **B.**   Reasonably neat: shoes and trainers in pairs; most items folded or hanging neat, but not in any particular order.

☐   **C.**   Simple; a small selection for my lifestyle, most items neatly hanging in groups whilst underwear, socks, tights and tops are less organised in drawers.

☐   **D.**   Organised in groups with underwear and hosiery in reasonable order; shoes on a rack or in boxes with shoe trees, out of season clothes in bags.

☐   **E.**   Efficiently sorted into groups and colours, a specific place for everything, wooden hangers, shoe trees and appropriate boxes for accessories.

☐   **F.**   Reasonably well organised in groups: all black together, colours possibly mixed up and a place for accessories, including hats.

☐   **G.**   Wardrobe full, but fairly well organised; not enough room for all the shoes. Drawers full of hosiery, coloured underwear and make-up.

☐   **H.**   Full of lots of the latest brands and accessories, with the latest trends the nearest to hand.

☐   **I.**   Several items, particularly tops, cardigans and jackets in several colours and a selection of shoes, jewellery and lots of make-up, all neat in boxes or drawers.

☐   **J.**   Several wardrobes: a hoarder; full with various styles, patterns and colours that are mixed together; drawers of accessories including coloured underwear.

4. What type of hairstyle do you prefer?

☐ **A.** A simple wash-and-go hairstyle, no fuss, visit hairdressers very irregularly.

☐ **B.** An easy to manage style, either short or can be tied up when exercising, but looks smart, attend a hairdresser as required.

☐ **C.** Short, clean, simple, neat style: attend hairdressers regularly to keep the shape.

☐ **D.** A sleek style, relying on a regular good cut, nothing fussy and stays in place all day, possibly with a few lowlights.

☐ **E.** A modern elegant hairstyle that looks stylish throughout the day or evening; kept in good condition by using products to keep the look and regular cut and highlights a must.

☐ **F.** A short sleek cut that makes a statement or shoulder length, well cut, possibly strong highlights or striking colour.

☐ **G.** Long or short in a lavish style that has texture and movement in my hair. Will spend time to look good and use several products to get the style; like changing the look with colour or cut.

☐ **H.** A popular style, with the latest cut/colour and products that always make it look up to the minute.

☐ **I.** Lots of texture and movement with highlights or change of colour; looks neat and feminine. I use products to give movement and to keep it in place; nothing sleek or straight.

☐ **J.** Something expressive, long, loose or short with movement, like striking colours or highlights; nothing neat and tidy.

5. What accessories do you buy?

❏ **A.** Practical and useful such as a watch, wooden or metal necklace, prefer scarves to jewellery, rucksack and mobile phone.

❏ **B.** Several sporty headgear items, rucksack and/or sports holdall, one or two plain necklaces and earrings for dressing up, plus a few handbags.

❏ **C.** A few simple items – a watch, silver/ gold necklace or handcrafted or rough stone beads, rucksack, black or brown small handbag.

❏ **D.** A small selection of simple items such as a good watch, neutral handbags, gold/silver necklace and several simple earrings, quality ring, a few modern necklaces to match outfits, plus a couple of scarves to wear with winter coat.

❏ **E.** Several quality designer costume jewellery of this season that complete or update outfits, nothing overpowering; quality scarves plus expensive rings with precious stones, best quality bracelets and necklaces for dressy occasions.

❏ **F.** Like to wear only a few bold items that that give a focal point that are up-to-date and can change my look, e.g. large brooch, a belt with a large buckle, big rings, dangly or diamond earrings, tattoos, bold sun glasses, oversized handbags, possibly several hats. Large hats especially for special events or weddings.

❏ **G.** Lots! A fetish for bags and shoes, like to buy on impulse and to change my look. Various belts, scarves, earrings and bracelets often several worn at the same time.

❏ **H.** The latest fashion fads – earrings, necklace, hats, belts, watches, tattoos, sun glasses and designer bags.

❏ **I.** Several items, dainty and colourful bracelets and necklaces, rings with coloured stones, fancy belts, coloured or sparkly watches, several coloured bags and shoes but avoid anything big and overpowering.

❏ **J.** A selection of unusual items from fairs, markets in antique gold or well worn items that can be adapted, handmade jewellery (e.g. handbags with fringes, ceramic bangles, well-loved antique pearls, decorative hair clips, drop earrings, fancy scarves, artistic bracelets, fancy buttons, belts and a variety of glasses).

6. What are your favourite colours?

❏ **A.** Earthy and natural tones blended
(e.g. sand, indigo, grey, browns, khaki, navy).

❏ **B.** Mostly neutral shades with a splash of colour
(e.g. black, navy, blue, white with red, blue or green).

❏ **C.** Prefer earthy shades blended together, nothing bright and garish
(e.g. soft navy, indigo, dusky blues, grey, sand, beige, khaki).

❏ **D.** Mostly neutrals and classic combinations
(e.g. navy or black with white, brown with cream plus mid-blues).

❏ **E.** Elegant monochromatic combinations or a dash of colour, nothing garish
or too bright
(e.g. camel with black or ivory; stone, taupe, pewter, soft navy,
olive with cream, coral or jade).

❏ **F.** Maximum contrast, bold colours; favourites black, white and red.

❏ **G.** Prefer passionate colours to neutrals such as reds, purples, violets, yellow/lemon,
blues, pinks.

❏ **H.** A variety of the season's colours plus black a favourite.

❏ **I.** Soft candy colours
(e.g. ice pink, lilac and white, with navy or grey, nothing dark and drab).

❏ **J.** Colours in vibrant shades that clash, nothing plain
(e.g. purples, yellows, reds together or pinks, and reds with blues).

7. What feel of fabrics and textures do you like?

❑ **A.** Natural fabrics and rough textures
(e.g. denim, hand knits, rib knits, linen, cords and cotton).

❑ **B.** Smooth fabrics and textures
(e.g. cotton, jersey cotton, denim, linen mix, spandex, nothing synthetic).

❑ **C.** Natural fabrics with some crisp texture
(e.g. natural finish wools, linen mix, crisp cotton, denim, alpaca).

❑ **D.** Mixture of fabrics that are smooth and don't crease
(e.g. brush cotton, viscose, elastane, fine wool, and tweeds).

❑ **E.** Soft fabrics with fine texture, some with synthetic fibres to keep them from creasing such as lycra or viscose fabrics
(e.g. cashmere, wool crepe, soft weave cotton, jersey, charmeuse, silk velvet, alpaca).

❑ **F.** Smooth rich fabrics with a crisp silhouette
(e.g. gabardine, worsted wools, crisp cotton, brocade, leather, suede and satin).

❑ **G.** Soft-feel fabrics, frills, with some synthetics for softness
(e.g. polycotton, velvet, cashmere, soft leather, lace, embroidery, organza, chiffon, velour, and silk).

❑ **H.** Various blends of fabrics and textures, according to the fashion but denim, cotton blends, fine wools; mixture of fabrics.

❑ **I.** Fine textures and fabrics
(e.g. fine wool, soft or brush cotton, velvet and jersey, chiffon, cashmere, lace, silk, embroidery, organza, sequins, chiffon).

❑ **J.** Mixture of fabrics and contrasting textures
(e.g. lycra to metallic, sequins, leather, silk, felts to velvet).

8. What skincare routine and make-up do you like wearing and how much?

☐ **A.** Don't usually wear it, possibly on special occasions and then only lip balm and mascara. Easy routine for my skin, soap and water quite often.

☐ **B.** Like to look natural so only lip gloss and mascara unless for dressing up then eye make-up. Simple and easy products for my skin and hair routine.

☐ **C.** Simple and easy skin routine with natural products, only lip balm and mascara for work or special occasions, otherwise nothing.

☐ **D.** A neat simple routine of foundation, powder, blusher, eye make-up, mascara and lipstick, nothing too garish, simple skin routine.

☐ **E.** I like to have good skin, have facials and apply a selection of high quality skin and make-up products with quality brushes. Like soft natural tones to suit me.

☐ **F.** I like a variety of skin products and try various treatments, my make-up either strong bold lips or eyes using a full selection of items and brushes. My nails have strong colours or a French manicure with long nails.

☐ **G.** I never go out without my make-up fully completed, I like a variety of shades of lipsticks, nail varnishes and eye shadows. Like facials and a good skin care routine.

☐ **H.** A selection of the season's shades in all the various products to give the up-to-the-minute looks including my nails. Regularly go to a nail bar and try a variety of skin routines.

☐ **I.** A full make-up, even in the garden, several choices of colours and a lipstick is the key. Skin routine and beauty treatments important.

☐ **J.** Skin routine hit and miss with several products. Either no make-up or apply according to my mood, the eyes are key whether the look is gothic or more for a dramatic colourful look.

9. Disaster! There is an emergency and you have 10 minutes to get your favourite items from the wardrobe. What would they be?

☐ **A.** A few items of casual wear – jeans, jumper, t-shirts, jacket, trainers and my most comfortable shoes.

☐ **B.** My favourite trainers, tracksuit, a few pairs of jeans, tops, jumper and outer jacket.

☐ **C.** My best trousers and jacket, a few pairs of jeans, few tops and cardigans/jumpers, comfortable and smart shoes.

☐ **D.** My latest trousers and skirt with matching jacket, coat, favourite jumper, cardigan and a few tops plus my best jewellery with my smartest navy and black shoes.

☐ **E.** My favourite designer coat, few jackets, trousers and skirts with some tops and a few pairs of shoes and my most expensive and favourite accessories.

☐ **F.** My favourite and boldest style shoes and accessories together with my favourite jeans, trousers, skirt and designer tops and jackets. A few hats.

☐ **G.** Panic! Love so much. My favourite skirts, pair of jeans or trousers and blouses with as many shoes, bags and jewellery as I can with a few fancy knickers, bras and some make-up.

☐ **H.** As many as I can from my favourite jeans, tops particularly this season's latest items and accessories.

☐ **I.** My favourite tops and skirts, best fitted jacket, jeans, and my favourite shoes, jewellery with some underwear and make-up.

☐ **J.** My latest creations, a selection of coloured tops, favourite shoes and boots with a few pairs of jeans, several accessories, underwear and make-up.

10. Which of these groups of famous women have a style nearest to yours? (You may not pick out the whole group as I have included various ages.)

☐ **A.** Charlie Dimmock, Ruth Kelly, Billie Piper, Jade Goody, Renee Zellweger, the late Anita Roddick (All have a very casual, relaxed, unfussy style).

☐ **B.** Cameron Diaz, Sally Gunnell, Denise Lewis, Paula Radcliffe, Sharon Davies, Gabby Logan (All have an athletic look with an informal sporty style).

☐ **C.** Yasmin Le Bon, Kate Moss, Nicole Kidman, Fiona Phillips, Helen Mirren, Kristin Scott Thomas, Angelina Jolie, Jennifer Aniston (All keep a naturally youthful slim physique; look neat and precise whether informal or formal).

☐ **D.** Sandra Bullock, Selina Scott, Countess of Wessex, Princess Anne, Angela Rippon, Hilary Clinton, Amanda Burton, Anna Ford, Chancellor Angela Merkel (All have a timeless style that is simple, co ordinated and traditional).

☐ **E.** Catherine Zeta Jones, Sue Barker, Lady Helen Taylor, Queen Noor of Jordan, Queen Rania of Jordan, the late Princess Diana and Jacqueline Kennedy Onassis (All always look very chic and elegant but the key is quality and simplicity).

☐ **F.** Madonna, Cher, Sharon Osborne, Tara Palmer-Tomkinson, Katie Andre (Jordan), Bette Midler (All like striking designs and a bold look which makes a statement).

☐ **G.** Emma Bunton, Liz Hurley, Lorraine Kelly, Martine McCutcheon, Jennifer Lopez, Beyonce, Stella McCartney, Elizabeth Taylor and Sophia Loren (All dress and look feminine and/or sexy with an air of lavishness about them).

☐ **H.** Victoria Beckham, Paris Hilton, Kate Moss, Colleen McCloughlin, WAGs (They change their style with the latest fashion of the season and many people love to follow their look).

☐ **I.** Barbara Windsor, Dolly Parton, Joan Rivers, Kylie Minogue, Bonnie Langford (They have a girlie baby-doll look and always appear youthful and full of energy).

☐ **J.** Kelly Osborne, Zandra Rhodes, Elizabeth Emanuel, Vivienne Westwood, Tina Turner (They all have an original style, different look each time and nothing conventional).

11. What is your home like?

☐ **A.** Functional and lived in. Simple plain walls with little soft furnishings; prefers plants or wooden ornaments, often untidy and can be full of hoarded items.

☐ **B.** Simple and unfussy with the bare essentials, functional modern soft furnishings, nothing too colourful or fussy, possibly some gym equipment.

☐ **C.** Simple, tidy and organised with occasional lapses in areas not of interest to you. Chunky wooden furniture, soft furnishings in neutral shades with mostly wooden or metal ornaments or candles.

☐ **D.** A neat and tidy home with a place for everything. Well co-ordinated with good quality soft furnishings in classic styles.

☐ **E.** Well designed, well maintained, very stylish with contemporary and classic furniture and original soft furnishings (e.g. paintings or sculptures).

☐ **F.** Big open rooms or open plan, items that make a statement. Large scale furniture and soft furnishings (e.g. large lamps, cushions and paintings, fruit bowls, vases, flowers and wine glasses).

☐ **G.** Furniture with soft ornate lines. A variety of home furnishings are important, such as several cushions, ornaments, curtains with fancy tags and drapes, candles, flowers in a variety of colours.

☐ **H.** Modern furniture and soft furnishings in up-to-the-minute season's colours by well known brands.

☐ **I.** Small rooms, neat and well presented, ornate furniture, a variety of soft furnishings from old to new which give colour and interest to the rooms.

☐ **J.** One that can be adapted and changed, new or second hand furniture that has been modified. Soft furnishings in various textures that are handmade or unusual shapes, mostly cluttered with a variety of items.

How to calculate your results

The moment of finding out your Wardrobe Personality is here. Simply count how many of each letter you have ticked and put the answer in the box below against the relevant letter.

My points:

A	B	C	D	E	F	G	H	I	J

The highest scoring letters will indicate which are your strongest Wardrobe Personalities.

If you answered:

Mostly **A** = your Wardrobe Personality is – **Casual**

Mostly **B** = your Wardrobe Personality is – **Sporty**

Mostly **C** = your Wardrobe Personality is – **Gamine**

Mostly **D** = your Wardrobe Personality is – **Classic**

Mostly **E** = your Wardrobe Personality is – **Chic Classic**

Mostly **F** = your Wardrobe Personality is – **Dramatic**

Mostly **G** = your Wardrobe Personality is – **Romantic**

Mostly **H** = your Wardrobe Personality is – **Fashion Fad**

Mostly **I** = your Wardrobe Personality is – **Ingénue**

Mostly **J** = your Wardrobe Personality is – **Creative**

• • • • •

"Keeping your clothes well pressed will keep you from looking hard pressed."

COLEMAN COX

CHAPTER FIVE

The 10 Wardrobe Personalities Explained

Having completed the questionnaire the next stage is to find out what your primary Wardrobe Personality is. In this chapter I will describe each of them, so you can see what this means for you. You should begin to see some of your own traits.

There is no right or wrong Wardrobe Personality. Each has its own unique features, benefits and disadvantages. As elsewhere in life, we tend to be tolerant of and relate to people like ourselves. Similarly, when people are different to us we may find their manner difficult to understand.

For example, a Casual is more likely to relate and empathise with another Casual, whereas a Classic is likely to find some of the appearance and behaviours of a Dramatic challenging and those of a Casual untidy, disorganised and too informal.

But this is a world full of differences and variety and it is helpful to remember this when dealing with people. When you recognise their Wardrobe Personality, it will help you to rationalise certain behaviours and styles, and maybe adjust yours accordingly.

Revealing your unique character

By choosing clothes, including the type of fabrics, styles and accessories that reflect our Wardrobe Personality, we reveal our inner selves, allowing our own unique personality to shine through. Such messages are very important as they indicate how people will perceive us, albeit subconsciously. Understanding your Wardrobe Personality will help you to appreciate how to wear your own individual styles so that you feel comfortable, confident and happy in yourself.

Of course, there may be times when you may want to behave differently, e.g. you may be quite conservative, but occasionally like to party with your friends. You may then want to be fashionable and dramatic. Knowing your Wardrobe Personality will enable you to adapt your wardrobe with a few inexpensive occasional items to use when you need them.

The questionnaire may have revealed that you are a combination of two personalities, predominantly one type, perhaps at work, with a second one more visible in your personal life. You may find you have aspects of one personality that you wish to develop further as you change through life experiences. Once you recognise what Wardrobe Personalities you fit into, you will be more aware of how you feel in certain clothes; of what makes you feel great and what does not. You will also start to identify the Wardrobe Personalities of your family, friends and colleagues.

(Note. The famous personalities I have used in this book are based on their image as portrayed in the media and not from my own personal experience. It is possible they may be quite different, if I were to meet them in their private lives.)

Wardrobe Personalities fall broadly into 10 categories. These are:
A. **Casual**
B. **Sporty**
C. **Gamine**
D. **Classic**
E. **Chic Classic**
F. **Dramatic**
G. **Romantic**
H. **Fashion Fad**
I. **Ingénue**
J. **Creative**

The circle Of Wardrobe Personalities

This diagram is to help you visualise the differences between the various Wardrobe Personalities such as the most informal (Casual), compared to the most formal (Chic Classic), or the very imaginative style (Creative). You can be a combination of any number of them, which is what makes you unique. This will be explained in more detail in Chapter 7.

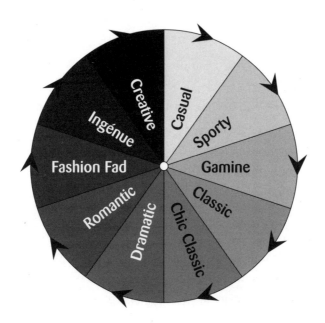

• • • • •

The Casual

What suggests her style:

The Casual likes comfort - nothing fancy or frilly for her! She likes to be practical and, of all the types, she has the least interest in clothes and fashion. To look professional, she will need to adopt good habits to achieve good grooming. She is very relaxed, easy-going and rarely gets annoyed. She is a person who likes informality and has a happy-go-lucky style. She likes unfussy clothes that give ease of movement and will not sacrifice comfort. She can easily underestimate time and turn up late for meetings/functions. She is always busy, trying to fit too much into a day. Organisation and planning are not her forte and she should consider setting up regimes and procedures to become more efficient when it matters. She focuses on what she wants and what she is trying to achieve, which may at times make her appear thoughtless. She probably enjoys reading, travel, computers, outdoor pursuits or being with animals. She is often intellectual and/or are generally happy to be involved in physical/manual work. She may work outdoors and is not afraid to get her hands dirty.

Some of the messages a Casual woman likes to give out:

Relaxed, self-assured, friendly, easy going, practical or intelligent and knowledgeable.

Famous names she may relate to:

Charlie Dimmock, Billie Piper, Sara Cox, Shirley Williams, Jade Goody, Renee Zellweger, Ruth Kelly and the late Anita Roddick.

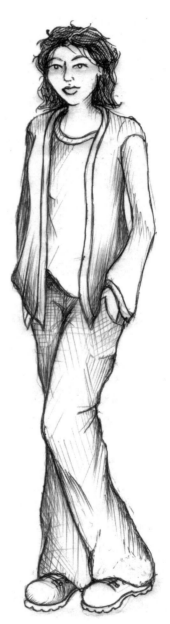

"The Casual is a person who likes informality and has a happy-go-lucky style. She likes unfussy clothes that give ease of movement and will not sacrifice comfort."

Traits of a Casual woman:

1. Prefers comfortable unfussy clothes with ease of movement. Likes layers and generally avoids fitted or fussy styles. Is more comfortable in casual wear than formal wear.
2. Slack with grooming and needs to adopt good habits to look smart.
3. Likes a wash-and-go hairstyle, easy to manage and no fuss.
4. Very few accessories, possibly a watch, a silver/gold chain or ethnic styles.
5. Likes shoes to be comfortable rather than fashionable, e.g. loafers, plain slip-ons, Velcro fastening trainers.
6. Likes fabrics made from natural fibres, e.g. wool, cotton, linen, denim, tweed, raw silk, rib knits and hand knits. Likes texture, such as knobbly fabrics and rough textures.
7. Likes plain materials or patterns such as checks, stripes, plaids, paisleys, but nothing bold.
8. Chooses earthy tone colours, nothing electric or bright.
9. A simple wardrobe of items she can layer and mix is the ideal.
10. Her home can be untidy and disorganised; she prefers travel to spending money on decorative accessories.
11. Rarely wears make-up, when she does it is mainly lip balm and mascara.

Possible hobbies:

Reading, computers, vegetable gardening, i.e. allotments, travelling (travels light!), walking, cycling, outdoor pursuits, dealing with pets or animals, attending rock concerts.

Possible professions:

Nurse, home help, gardener, GP, vet or otherwise working with animals, agricultural pursuits, police, IT expert, teacher, physiotherapist, professor, MP or councillor, journalist or actor.

Areas for a Casual to think about:

A Casual needs to be aware of her appearance and accept that it does have an important impact on her overall personal image which will influence how successful she may be, both in her personal and working life, particularly if she works in formal business. Failure to accept this may result in a Casual not achieving her full potential or being overlooked for promotion. The level of action required will depend upon her career, how ambitious she is and on the type of job. In these cases, it may help a Casual to bring greater emphasis to her secondary Wardrobe Personality (see Chapter 6). On the positive side, her relaxed, friendly manner can lighten up people's attitude and approach. What's more, Casuals can be more confident than others as they don't worry too much about detail and prefer to look at the bigger picture.

Personal image tips:

- Establish a set routine to achieve a good standard of grooming, particularly for important occasions.
- Ensure clothes are ironed, use dry cleaners if necessary to ensure you have sufficient items for the week.
- Make a conscious effort to shop for a smart wardrobe of clothes for work or going out with the children, and which suit your lifestyle; a personal shopper will give you ideas and suggestions.
- Buy good quality shoes and bags for a professional look and keep them clean to look groomed and stylish.

Understand other Wardrobe Personalities:

- Recognise that some people (e.g. Gamines, Classics) like efficiency and detail; they will expect more information and accuracy than Casuals sometimes deliver.
- Try to organise your time and respect others; particularly when it involves keeping people waiting, getting the children to school or events, or meeting deadlines for crucial projects.
- When sharing a home with non-Casuals you will need to appreciate that they may find you untidy.

Team player:

- A Casual adds value to a team as she has a relaxed, friendly manner and rarely gets perturbed.
- Good with IT, animals or children; not afraid of physical or dirty work.
- Generally sees the big picture and works quickly.

The Sporty

What suggests her style:

The Sporty likes to look fit, keep energetic and wear unfussy clothes that offer ease of movement. She likes to look relaxed, but smart. (She is smarter than a Casual, but more informal than a Classic). She likes to keep a youthful shape, is weight-conscious and will keep in trim by playing sport or exercising. She has a confident manner and a carefree attitude, although she can be impatient as she is always busy and on the go. She is determined and focused on what she wants to achieve, which may sometimes make her appear self-centred, although she can be a good team player. She enjoys having fun and being adventurous. She will try various sports throughout her life.

Some of the messages a Sporty woman likes to give out:

Confident, active, smart, fit, youthful, and innovative.

Famous names she may relate to:

Denise Lewis, Sally Gunnell, Cameron Diaz, Gabby Logan, Sharon Davies, Kelly Homes.

"The Sporty has a confident manner and a carefree attitude, although she can be impatient as she is always busy and on the go."

Traits of a Sporty woman:

1. Likes simple, relaxed clothes that show her fit physique. Prefers relaxed casual wear, but likes to look smart for work if formal wear is required or for special occasions.
2. Her grooming can be a bit hit and miss due to lack of time.
3. Her hair must be easy to manage but well cut.
4. Have few accessories – a watch, plain gold/silver chain, a black or brown handbag, rucksack and gym bag.
5. Likes shoes that are modern, plain and comfortable e.g. designer trainers, sneakers or slip-ons, flat boots.
6. Likes fabrics that are natural or have stretch, e.g. cotton, denim, wool and linen, lycra and spandex. Avoids soft-feel fussy fabrics.
7. Prefers plain materials to patterns, dislikes big bold detail.
8. Likes earthy or subdued colours, nothing garish.
9. Likes a wardrobe with a good selection of items she can layer, adapt and mix to suit her lifestyle.
10. Prefers a simple, functional home with unfussy furniture and few home accessories. Prefers gadgets to fancy ornaments and accessories.
11. A simple make-up, for dressing up, such as lip gloss, mascara and possibly some eye make-up.

Possible hobbies:

A variety of sports, going to the gym, modern music, travelling, movies.

Possible professions:

Personal trainer, sports commentator, gym teacher, events organiser, armed forces, head hunter, money broker, finance, entrepreneur, foreign exchange dealer, TV personality, IT to business management.

(Some people may have this Wardrobe Personality in their personal life as a secondary Wardrobe Personality – see Chapter 6.)

Areas for a Sporty to think about:

A Sporty needs to appreciate that although she is a confident and a focused person, particularly with sport, not everyone is so interested or has her drive and energy. Other people have enthusiasm for other things such as the arts, science or reading.

Personal image tips:

- In professional business, be aware you will require a structured and smart appearance (e.g. shoes and hair should be kept in a businesslike style).
- Keep an eye on your grooming, slack grooming is an indication you lack attention to detail.
- Concentrate on your business wardrobe as well as your casual, and update as required. If you are a mum at home, don't neglect looking smart when out and about.

Understand other Wardrobe Personalities:

- Playing sports helps you to gain confidence and mix with others, but appreciate that others may not be so sociable and may not have your self-esteem.
- Be aware that some people prefer a more creative or stylish appearance, as their interests are more arty or conservative than yours.

Team player:

- A Sporty adds value to a team, as she generally likes working as part of a team, although she can be very competitive.
- A Sporty will push the boundaries, if she thinks it necessary, to achieve the desired result, as she always wants to win.
- Energy and competitiveness can encourage others in the team, but don't overpower them.
- Will go for things and not worry too much about the small detail.

The Gamine

What suggests her style:

The Gamine is generally a combination of Casual or Sporty and Classic. Her style is simple and she is not keen on fussy clothes. She looks neat and compact even in a simple pair of jeans and a T-shirt. She may be a tomboy when young. She is busy, with boundless energy. Generally, she will be a person with a small frame, often has a long neck and is evenly proportioned. She will retain her physical shape even as she ages or straight after having a baby. She doesn't always understand why others can easily put on weight. She is good with detail and likes things to be perfect, particularly when it is something that interests her. She can be very focused on one thing and take her time with projects. She needs to realise that being exact all the time can cause stress and that others can become bored with too much detail. She likes to get her own way, is generally determined and can be obstinate.

Messages she likes to give out:

Detailed, neat, energetic, competent, accurate.

Famous names she may relate to:

Kate Moss, Angelina Jolie, Yasmin Le Bon, Jennifer Aniston, Fiona Phillips, Nicole Kidman, Meg Ryan, Helen Mirren, Kristin Scott Thomas and the late Audrey Hepburn.

"The Gamine is busy, with boundless energy. Generally, she will be a person with a small frame, often has a long neck and is evenly proportioned."

Traits of a Gamine woman:

1. Wears neat and small-scale clothes, often slim-fit and needs to avoid loose and chunky items. Likes comfortable clothes that are unfussy.
2. Good grooming can easily be obtained, due to her small neat physique, but remember to clean shoes!
3. Has a wash-and-go hairstyle and will keep it short.
4. Likes only a few accessories, often only a watch.
5. Chooses shoes that are practical and comfortable rather than fashionable, e.g. heavy soled lace-ups and plain slip ons.
6. Likes fabrics in natural fibres, e.g. fine wool, cotton, linen mix, brushed cotton, fine cords and denim. Stiff crisp fabrics are the best.
7. Likes plain or small-scale patterns; nothing big and bold.
8. Chooses earthy or subdued tones in preference to strong bright colours.
9. Her wardrobe has a small selection of clothes that are adaptable to suit her lifestyle. She replaces clothes when they are worn out and dislikes too many options to choose from.
10. Has a tidy home with occasional lapses, prefers hand finished solid wood furnishings and simple home accessories, nothing fancy or ornate.
11. Little or no make-up, lip balm and mascara.

Possible hobbies:

'Singleton' sports such as golf, climbing, cycling, walking, fencing, running, swimming, IT, reading, detail painters (i.e. maps, scenery).

Possible professions:

Gamines can be in various professions where attention to detail is required, with many of their chosen careers based on their secondary Wardrobe Personality. Fashion model, air stewardess, television entertaining or presenting (ideal as their body shape stays slim), actor, journalist, forensic science, editor, graphic designer, copywriter, surgeon, solicitor, finance, personal trainer, landscape gardener, interior designer, hairdresser, printer.

Areas for a Gamine to think about:

A Gamine should appreciate that she is fortunate with her weight and that not everyone has a small frame or can stay slim all her life. Her propensity to worry about the slightest detail can also lead to her taking longer than necessary to make a decision; this will be particularly evident when shopping for clothes, organising the home or planning family events. She likes things that interest her to be perfect, but needs to remember what is perfect to her may not be the same for others. Life is not perfect and nor are we, so she should not become stressed about it. A Gamine should question whether it is more important to focus on being effective or efficient.

Personal image tips:
- Wear slim fitted jeans and trousers, skirts and jackets. Loose baggy clothes will drown you.
- Wear smaller patterns or solids to suit your small scale.
- You'll look good in formal and informal wear.
- Add colour to give interest to your look, otherwise you can look boring to others.

Understand other Wardrobe Personalities:
- Other people can find too much detail boring and they will sometimes appreciate and benefit from being given the 'big picture' or some creativity.
- You are often extreme, obsessive about neatness or what suits or interests you, but slack about what does not. Take time and effort to consider other people's interests when sharing a house or office.

Team player:
- Be aware that some people prefer a more creative or stylish appearance, as their interests are more arty or conservative than yours.
- Great for spotting the details and presenting a precise project or presentation.

The Classic

What suggests her style:

The Classic has a conventional and timeless style; she is always neat and well presented. She prefers quality rather than quantity, and style to fashion. She always wants good value for money and chooses classical simple styles which look great on her, but which others may consider boring or traditional. She has a conservative attitude, often speaks quietly and does not seek undue attention. Conversely, a Classic can be overlooked if she does not speak out or learn to praise herself. A good planner and organiser, she likes familiarity and does not rush into change; wanting first to consider all the reasons why change is needed. Keeps her home well organised.

Messages she likes to give out:

Competent, reliable, trustworthy, organised, professional.

Famous names she may relate to:

Sandra Bullock, Laura Bush, Princess Caroline of Monaco, Anna Walker, Ffion Hague, Moira Stuart, Anna Ford, Countess of Wessex, Jacqui Smith MP, Chancellor Angela Merkel.

"**The Classic always wants good value for money and chooses classical simple styles which look great on her, but which others may consider boring or traditional.**"

Traits of a Classic woman:

1. A simple co-ordinated wardrobe to suit her life style. Finds a casual wardrobe more difficult as she prefers a tailored look; prefers casual trousers to jeans. Likes clothes to fit well and prefers value for money to fashion.
2. Grooming is generally tidy, smart and practical.
3. Needs hair to be neat; relies on an excellent cut with a neat finish.
4. Accessories will be simple and co ordinate with her outfit, e.g. toned-in necklace, quality watch, silver or gold necklace.
5. Shoes are simple; plain loafers, court shoes, small heel or flat boots in black or brown leather.
6. Likes fabrics with fine textures, such as jersey, soft weave cotton, worsteds, fine wool and tweeds some with added synthetic fibres for smoothness and neatness, e.g. Lycra, polyamide and elastane.
7. Prefers plain or small patterns, such as checks, herringbone and paisley.
8. Has a high proportion of neutral colours in her wardrobe, e.g. grey, black, navy or brown.
9. Likes purchasing items from one brand/designer to achieve a successful co-ordinated look.
10. Likes her home to be simple and stylish, well organised with a place for everything. Furnishings to be practical and of good quality and matching look.
11. Likes her make-up to be well applied with a simple routine and to give a modest look.

Possible hobbies:

Golf, tennis, sailing, walking, Girl Guides/Brownies leader, wine, classical or popular music, visiting museums or National Trust properties.

Possible professions:

Banker, solicitor, accountant, officer in armed forces, surgeon, project manager, supervisor and leaders, forensics, project manager, consultant, committee leaders.

Areas for a Classic to think about:

She needs to be wary of staying in a rut. The Classic is well organised – the type of person who makes lists and plans ahead. She finds it easy to have a co-ordinated and organised wardrobe, but is less comfortable with casual wear or dressing for informal events.

Personal image tips:

- You will generally have well established grooming routines, but don't let them lapse if you are in an informal environment or on casual days.
- Don't stick to the same shops year-in, year-out, check out new ones and try alternative brands.
- Update your image with simple tops or accessories, such as a necklace or scarf.
- Business casual: make sure you wear casual shoes not your business shoes!
- For casual wear, go for simple structures, styles and less formal fabrics that are comfortable and still look neat; otherwise you can look sloppy and unkempt.
- Presentation skills training will benefit you, as you do not naturally like attention.

Understand other Wardrobe Personalities:

- Appreciate that some people are not natural organisers and are better at ideas and starting projects than following them through to completion.
- Whereas you like consistency, be aware that other personalities enjoy change and constantly like fresh or new ideas. It is perfectly acceptable to question why change is needed but be ready to adopt new ideas in order to keep current and to move with the times.

Team player:

- You are a great asset to a team as you add value by providing structure, planning and organisation.
- You do not look for the limelight and are more concerned with the job being done correctly.
- You're a good time keeper, chairman of meetings or captain of teams.

The Chic Classic

What suggests her style:

The Chic Classic is stylish, elegant and sophisticated with a self-assured attitude. She likes simple classic styles yet with a touch of modern elegance. She succeeds in the skill of constantly being well dressed, well mannered, and carries herself with poise and elegance. She has a graceful style with a touch of individuality. She can appear modest, but can easily generate presence when she walks into a room by looking so stylish and well turned-out and, inevitably, exuding inner confidence. She has a strong interest in clothes, insisting on excellence and will pay for what she wants, favouring quality over quantity. She will have a wardrobe built up over many seasons that will provide numerous opportunities for mixing and matching. The Chic Classic is probably the most admired for her style by others, however, some Wardrobe Personalities (Casuals, Creatives) may regard her as too prim and proper.

Messages she likes to give out:

Professional, elegant, well mannered, efficient, reliable, trustworthy, polished, organised.

Famous names she may relate to:

Catherine Zeta Jones, Sue Barker, Queen Rania of Jordan, Queen Noor of Jordan, Lady Helen Taylor, Kate Middleton, the late Princess Diana and Jacqueline Kennedy Onasis.

"The Chic Classic can appear modest, but can easily generate presence when she walks into a room by looking so stylish and well turned-out."

Traits of a Chic Classic woman:

1. Likes contemporary elegant styles that are timeless and must be well made and well designed. Nothing body hugging or big and baggy.
2. Her grooming is always meticulous.
3. Her hair is simple, modern, neat and nothing fussy but in good condition.
4. Likes stylish modern accessories of very good quality that add to and change her looks.
5. Shoes will be of the highest quality she can afford, with a modern style and a selection for her lifestyle.
6. Likes fabrics that are soft with fine texture, some with synthetic fibres to keep them from creasing such as lycra or polyester, cashmere, soft wool and angora, wool crepe, jersey, leather, brush cotton, fine tweed.
7. Prefers plain or simple patterns.
8. Prefers colours to be monochromatic with a dash of rich colour, never too bright or showy. Neutrals will preferably be soft navy, taupe, camel or pewter.
9. Has a well-organised wardrobe, with high quality classic pieces and modern accessories that create a highly polished look.
10. Likes to have a stylish home with a mixture of classic and contemporary furnishings, with original paintings and sculptures. Likes everything in spotless condition.
11. Her make-up is of good quality, and she has a full, simple daily routine that is up to date and gives a highly polished look.

Possible hobbies:

Classical and/or modern music, wine, cuisine, ballet, opera, fashion, hosting social events/parties.

Possible professions:

Business professional, fashion retail management, business owner, classic actors, diplomat, events organiser.

Areas for a Chic Classic to think about:

The Chic Classic always likes to look stylish and hates looking unkempt, but she needs to be aware that others may find her intimidating. She should not be surprised when others turn up at events, either less formally dressed or sporting a higher fashion than her.

Personal image tips:

- You're generally considered the most stylish of the Wardrobe Personalities, so your only real problem may be toning down your appearance at very informal or casual events, e.g. pop concerts, sports events.
- Ignore high fashion magazine tips for shopping. Cheap trendy shops are not for you you will be uncomfortable in their clothes.
- Avoid extreme styles of accessories as they will overpower the look you wish to achieve.
- Presentation skills training will be a benefit, as you like everything to be correct.

Understanding other Wardrobe Personalities:

- Understand that some people are not as sophisticated and well mannered as you.
- Appreciate others for who they are and recognise that some people are not naturally stylish or as au fait with etiquette.

The Dramatic

What suggests her style:

The Dramatic has a strong personality and a presumptuous, innovative and sophisticated style. Very theatrical, oozing with confidence, she walks into a room with self-assurance and individuality and she likes to be noticed. She is, undoubtedly, conscious of looking good and, if she is interested in fashion, will like to lead with trends. New ideas come naturally to her and she will push new projects forward; she can be a starter, but not necessarily a finisher, so if in a team, she will need to be paired with other Wardrobe Personalities to ensure the project is completed. The Dramatic is a personality type that has a short attention span and is easily bored. She is someone who likes to be in charge, but does not take to authority; she likes the last word. The Dramatic has a powerful personality; she can be intimidating, sometimes appears arrogant and will focus on what she wants.

Messages she likes to give out:

Confident, self-assured, positive, authoritative, individual, innovative.

Famous names she may relate to:

Cher, Bette Midler, Madonna, Paris Hilton, Jerry Hall, Katie Price (Jordan), Vanessa Feltz, Sharon Osbourne.

"The Dramatic is very theatrical, oozing with confidence, she walks into a room with self-assurance and individuality and she likes to be noticed."

Traits of a Dramatic woman:

1. Likes clothes that are a bold sophisticated style, favours extremes, nothing average. Likes to make a statement with dramatic proportions, e.g. oversized coat, very short skirt or shorts.
2. Takes an interest in looking good and being well groomed.
3. Will have a long hairstyle or a short sharp neat structured style using hair products if necessary.
4. Enjoys wearing accessories that are bold, extravagant and oversized, such as fashionable large earrings or necklaces and oversized bags. Loves hats any excuse to wear them, large ones for weddings and Ascot!
5. Likes shoes that make a statement whether in style or colour. They will be kept in good condition.
6. Likes stiff fabrics with a firm finish, such as crisp cotton, silk, smooth wools, jerseys, gabardine, satin, or brocade for evening.
7. Prefers plain material to patterns, nothing fussy. If she chooses patterned, it will be stripes, checks or something arty.
8. Likes strong colours to achieve the desired effect: black and red are probably a favourite.
9. Likes a variety of clothes that make an impact at all occasions.
10. For the home – likes large rooms or an open plan style; oversized furnishings and big furniture, from big flowers in large vases to huge wine glasses.
11. Likes her make-up in strong colours either on the lips or eyes, adventurous.

Possible hobbies:

Sports (mainly team sports), travel, modern music, amateur dramatics, theatre, movies and fashion.

Possible professions:

Sales, telephone sales, events organisers, celebrities, entertainers, actors, dancers, barrister, head hunters, comedian. (More than most other Wardrobe Personalities, Dramatics may be in any career based on their secondary Wardrobe Personality, as long as it provides them with the necessary attention).

Areas for a Dramatic to think about:

A Dramatic is always keen to change and have new ideas, but you should remember that others are not always as ready. You can sometimes come across as arrogant and over-boisterous to some people; often you are keener to talk than to listen.

Personal image tips:

- Dramatics like strong colours, but ensure they are the correct shades to suit you; pick the boldest in your palette.
- A smile can break the ice and using humour will help people to warm to you.
- Depending on the occasion (e.g. business meeting with subordinates) tone down the bold authoritative appearance, without sacrificing your personality. You will achieve more open and honest communication.
- Don't buy a complete look from one brand or try to be too co-ordinated. Bring together items from a variety of designers and express your own style.

Understanding other Wardrobe Personalities:

- Appreciate that others may have a more conservative attitude, behaviour and appearance than you.
- Dramatics may see their outgoing personality as the life and soul of the party, but need to be conscious of stifling other people. Take time to show interest in others.
- You are a woman of extremes and moods; you readily express your views, but need to consider other people's feelings and views too.

Team player:

- Great for initiating ideas and generating energy and enthusiasm on new projects, but may need to show patience with others who need more time to digest ideas.
- Will lose interest if projects go on for some time, so involve another Wardrobe Personality (Classic or Gamine) to ensure it is planned and completed appropriately.

The Romantic

What suggests her style:

The Romantic likes to feel feminine and pretty. She loves clothes and likes to be aware of fashion. She always needs to look good to feel good. A Romantic will pay attention to the overall style of her outfit and to her accessories, especially her shoes and handbag; she cannot have enough of them. She is sociable and receptive, enjoys company and meeting new people, is easy to talk to and has a friendly personality. She will often flirt in a friendly way, being very comfortable in the company of men. When speaking she will often express herself with her hands. She generally has creative hobbies, e.g. cooking, the arts or music, and is passionate about whatever she does in life.

Famous names she may relate to:

Emma Bunton, Judy Finnigan, Linda Barker, Lorraine Kelly, Louise Rednapp, Jennifer Lopez, Sophia Loren, Martine McCutcheon, Fern Britten, Rula Lenska, Tamzin Outhwaite and the late Marilyn Monroe.

Messages she likes to give out:

Passionate, sophisticated, fun, sociable, caring, flirtatious, creative.

"A Romantic will pay attention to the overall style of her outfit and to her accessories, especially her shoes and handbag; she cannot have enough of them."

Traits of a Romantic woman:

1. Loves clothes. Likes soft flowing or voluptuous fitted clothes that make her feel feminine, nothing plain or neutral in colour for you. Enjoys evening wear.
2. Grooming is important, as she loves her clothes to look good.
3. Likes hair that has movement, either long or short fashionable styles and uses hair products.
4. Enjoys lots of accessories to give a extravagant effect from loop or drop earrings, bracelet, brooches, belts and will wear several at a time, e.g. couple of necklaces, bracelet and or brooch.
5. Has an obsession with shoes and will have lots! All with some pretty detail, sling backs, peep toes, wedges, high to kitten heel. Prefers heels to flat.
6. Prefers fine soft fluid or rich fabrics which have a soft feel including synthetics, polycotton, luxury cotton, velvet, cashmere, lightweight wool, silk, crinkle finish satin, velour, broderie anglaise, organza and lace.
7. Likes plain and patterns in florals, spots, soft blended plaids or checks.
8. Loves rich colours, preferring them to neutrals.
9. Enjoys a full wardrobe of clothes and accessories, with a touch of sensuous luxury (e.g. luxury cotton shirts, velvet jackets and expensive handmade shoes or cashmere coats).
10. Her home is important to her, with lots of colour and soft furnishings (sculptures, paintings, candles, cut glass), flowers in the home or garden and pots on the patio.
11. Loves her make-up and never goes without it. She has lots: her lipstick mascara, foundation, blusher and eyes are all important.

Possible hobbies:

Cooking, the arts; popular music (from pop, country, rock and reggae) painting, clothes, shopping, fashion, flower gardening, flower arranging, socialising.

Possible professions:

Entrepreneur, acting, television presenter, hairdresser, clothes retailer, stylists, beautician, image consultant, dressmaker, air stewardess, make-up artist or retailer, aromatherapist, musician, and author (romantic novels).

(Many people in caring or manual professions have this Wardrobe Personality in their personal life (secondary Wardrobe Personality) e.g. doctor, police officer, citizens advice counsellor, aromatherapist; pilates, yoga and personal trainer.

Areas for a Romantic to think about:

A Romantic is always passionate about what she believes in, but should be aware that not everyone will share her enthusiasm. She is keen to look and feel good, and is prepared to spend time to achieve this, but will need to remember others are not always so interested or as keen about their own appearance.

Personal image tips:

- Romantics always need a bigger wardrobe and more accessories than most other Wardrobe Personalities. You will benefit from organising items by colour and garment type.
- Try to plan your wardrobe for the season so that you spend less and have the clothes to suit your lifestyle.
- Continue to enjoy and love your accessories, try to plan what you need to go with what, but include an easy way to update or change your wardrobe as you like variety.
- Remember, what you see in a magazine may not necessarily feel comfortable on you, particularly if it is an inappropriate style for your body shape or in the wrong fabrics for your Wardrobe Personality.

Understand other Wardrobe Personalities:

Other Wardrobe Personalities may have a more conservative or less creative attitude to appearance and prefer relaxed or simple plain clothes; accept them for their style.

Team Player:

- You have creative ideas and like diversity, so you can improve the look of a presentation, documents or bring a completely different angle to a problem.
- Working with people such as Classics will help you to provide structure to your work, as you can be a butterfly, flitting all over the place owing to your creative and original thoughts and ideas.
- Your passion and enthusiasm can be infectious and inspire team members.

The Fashion Fad

What suggests her style:

The Fashion Fad likes to wear the latest trends, is always enthusiastic about the new craze, and is fixated with clothes. Celebrities are her icons. Quality is not the key thing for her, as she likes change and is keen to be a follower of fashion. She regularly buys magazines, watches the media awards, sees who is the latest pop or film star and follows what they wear. She loves shopping, checking out the latest brands, is conscious of her figure and tries to keep slim. Being happy means being up to date and looking trendy. However, this may not always work, as she will wear clothes that may look good on someone else, but not on her. She needs to try to bring out the best of who she truly is.

She enjoys having fun and is friendly but can be insecure and not always confident enough to develop her own style. She enjoys socialising and going out.

Messages she likes to give out:

Up-to-the-minute, trendy, fashionable, cool, sexy.

Famous names she may relate to:

Victoria Beckham, Isabella Harvey, Chantelle Houghton, Colleen McCloughlin, WAGs, Kate Moss.

"The Fashion Fad
regularly buys
magazines, watches the
media awards, sees
who is the latest pop
or film star and follows
what they wear."

Traits of a Fashion Fad woman:

1. Likes to wear the latest styles from informal to formal looks. Does not opt for the traditional style or a co-ordinated wardrobe. Being seen and admired in the latest trend is important to her.
2. Grooming is important as she cares about her looks, but this can get overlooked, particularly when the fashion is a relaxed look.
3. Likes her hair to be up-to-date and in the latest styles and colours.
4. Have the season's newest accessories, from the latest sunglasses, spectacles and headwear to rings, earrings, necklaces and bracelets.
5. Likes to have the latest shoes or trainers in the most popular brands, often reflecting her secondary Wardrobe Personality, e.g. Dramatic, Romantic or Sporty.
6. Loves fabrics that are in for the season, which will be influenced by what suits her secondary Wardrobe Personality, e.g. linen or satin, denim or cotton.
7. Materials and patterns are more likely to be plain, but if florals or abstracts are in fashion she will experiment with them.
8. Loves most colours, with black probably one of her favourite neutrals.
9. Has a full and overflowing wardrobe.
10. Her home is likely to be modern or updated with lavish modern soft furnishings.
11. She likes to experiment with her make-up, from the latest eye or lip colours to a strong or soft look.

Possible hobbies:

The arts, pop music, fashion, TV soaps, reality shows, movies, clothes shopping and keeping fit.

Possible professions:

Beautician, fashion retailer, dressmaker, stylist, sales. Any profession involving people and socialising.

Areas for a Fashion Fad to think about:

You think it is important to be trendy and in fashion and enjoy the variety of looks and various changes, but not everyone cares or has any interest in fashion.

With your knowledge and interest in fashion use the information to bring out your Secondary Wardrobe personality – the real you.

Personal image tips:

- A Fashion Fad can eventually mature into a Romantic, but failing that, they may end up dressing too young for their age.
- You can spend too much money keeping up with the trends; planning and adapting your wardrobe would save money.
- You can become a fashion victim and may end up looking trendy, but not stylish.
- Consider how to create an up-to-date look with your accessories, to save cost and make more use of the core items in your wardrobe, by purchasing some items that will last in fashion for several seasons.
- Pick up ideas from magazines and create a style that is truly you.

Understand other Wardrobe Personalities:

- Appreciate that some people like to be more conservative or casual than fashion conscious in their appearance.

Team player:

- You are generally a caring person, passionate about enjoying life and will include others.
- You are a person who likes to be liked and will try to fit in with the crowd.
- Your interest in fashion can help projects to have a modern or up-to-date look or fresh ideas.

The Ingénue

What suggests her style:

An Ingénue looks youthful, dainty and often appears very girlish or childlike. She is small framed with delicate features and can display feminine innocence. She likes to look pretty and dress colourfully (like a doll). She loves attention and may appear vain. She is often quite theatrical and flamboyant, and is full of energy, always on the go with a lively nature. An Ingénue likes to have her own way and can be impish, but with a sparkle in her eye that enables her to win people over. She is likely to either be in a creative profession or enjoy hobbies in the theatre, music or the arts. She will keep her physical shape throughout her life, even just after having a baby; as she matures she may evolve into a more sophisticated Romantic.

Messages she likes to give out:

Creative, gentle, gracious, glamourous and flirtatious.

Famous names she may relate to:

Barbara Windsor, Bonnie Langford, Dolly Parton, Kylie Minogue, Jennifer Ellison, Debbie Reynolds, Joan Rivers.

"The Ingénue is often quite theatrical and flamboyant, and is full of energy, always on the go with a lively nature."

Traits of an Ingénue woman:

1. Clothes always look neat, gently flowing with feminine lines or figure hugging with fancy detail, nothing baggy or chunky.
2. Spends time on her grooming, from washing her hair to applying her make-up. She always likes to look neat and girlie even when working in the garden or doing housework.
3. Likes a soft feminine look, often a curly hairstyle, nothing straight or unruly.
4. Loves her accessories, likes fancy detail, nothing heavy or plain, e.g. bows in her hair, fancy hair band or glittery jewellery.
5. Loves her shoes and enjoys her heels, must have details or colour, e.g. pink stilettos, fancy lace boots, sparkly evening shoes.
6. Likes fine textures and smooth fabrics; nothing heavy, e.g. fine wool, silk, satin, soft Jacquards, broderie anglaise, veiling / dress net in assorted colours, lace edging, embroidery silks, cotton, velvet and jersey.
7. Likes small-scale patterns, such as dots, small stripes, flowers, spots, softly blended plaids and checks.
8. Enjoys colour from baby pink to lilac, blues and poppy, she will generally avoid neutrals.
9. Prefers a wardrobe with good quality basics, such as skirts, dresses and fitted jackets. Lots of tops and blouses in a variety of colours or patterns to give variety.
10. Likes a compact home with lots of character, ornate furniture and lots of soft furnishings in various colours.
11. Enjoys experimenting with her make-up using colours to tone in with her clothes, must wear a full make-up everyday.

Possible hobbies:

The arts, ballet, dancing, popular music, painting, photography, fashion, floristry or flower gardening, clothes, shopping, fashion.

Possible professions:

Stage performer, ballet, dancer, actor, romantic writer, art dealer, make-up artist, clothing retail, florist.

Areas for an Ingénue to think about:

An Ingénue will need to be aware that not everyone enjoys paying as much attention to dress: to a Casual or Sporty it is time that could be better spent doing something else. The time an Ingénue spends on herself may be considered by others to be excessive and a sign of vanity. She has a youthful look all her life, but needs to avoid becoming obsessive about remaining youthful.

Personal image tips:

- From a career perspective, if an Ingénue wants to be in a profession with authority (apart from the arts), she may need to consider bringing attention to her secondary Wardrobe Personality or, at least, toning down her more youthful and flamboyant style. Consider more neutral shades for the key pieces.
- Keep your wardrobe organised and in colour order so that you know what you have in it.
- Plan and organise your wardrobe so as not to overspend on too many accessories.

Understanding other Wardrobe Personalities:

- Recognise you have naturally youthful physique whilst some other Wardrobe Personalities are less fortunate in keeping their shape as they get older.
- Appreciate that other Wardrobe Personalities may have little interest in style and fashion.
- Appreciate that others may think it very vain and time-wasting to care so much about your appearance and feel that there are more important things in life, although not to you.

Team player:

- You care about others and will involve people in your ideas.
- You can add flair by changing an uninteresting project into a colourful and interesting collage.
- Your energy and enthusiasm can influence others.

The Creative

What suggests her style:

The Creative is a person who likes a very individual look and may often be regarded as eccentric. She likes to express her artistic style, often with a different look each day. She has no interest in conforming to a traditional look. The Creative loves to experiment with her clothes, hair and accessories. She may design and make her own clothes, buy from markets, charity shops or use friends' and family's cast-offs to experiment and adapt her styles. The Creative loves vintage clothes and will re-invent them. She will experiment to get different effects. She can sometimes appear outlandish and a bit of a hippy.

Famous names she may relate to:

Vivienne Westwood, Kelly Osborne, Tina Turner, Toyah Wilcox, Elizabeth Emanuel, Miriam Margolyes and Zandra Rhodes.

Messages she likes to give out:

Adventurous, fun, unique, spontaneous, exciting, flirtatious.

"The Creative loves to experiment with her clothes, hair and accessories. She may design and make her own clothes, buy from markets and charity shops."

Traits of a Creative woman:

1. Likes a mixture of unusual looks from eccentric to bold and colourful. Dislikes anything classical or structured. Likes patterned trousers, fancy shirts, unusual ties, embroidered waistcoats – neon to ethnic. Enjoys flamboyant eveningwear with fancy accessories.
2. Grooming can seem unkempt as anything in style won't appeal and she must look unusual.
3. Hairstyles may be long and possibly messy; she loves to experiment with hair colour!
4. Loves unusual accessories, e.g. colourful belts, fancy blouses, scarves, patterned skirts and waistcoats and hats.
5. Loves her footwear, from coloured or unusual style shoes to heavy style biker boots; plain black shoes are not for her.
6. Favourite fabrics with include a mixture of contrasting textures from Lycra, metallic, satin, leather, silk, felts and velvet.
7. Lots of patterns to mismatch a mixture of designs.
8. Likes strong, bold colours, nothing soft and blended.
9. Her wardrobe has to have enough variety to change the look for each occasion.
10. Her home is important to her and she likes to change and adapt the look with a variety of soft furnishings, paintings or adding extras that give the desired look. She may buy second hand then adapt the furniture.
11. She loves to experiment and use various colours; the eyes are the focus.

Possible hobbies:

Music, fashion, artist, interior or fashion design, cooking, comedy, craft events, antiques fairs and market stalls.

Possible professions:

Musician, artist, clothes or interior designer, performer, actor, florist, merchandise display artist.

Areas for a Creative to think about:

A Creative will need to be aware that not everyone shares her interest in colour and her variety of ideas. Her appearance may, at times, be a little whacky (as may her ideas) to, e.g., a Casual, Sporty or Classic person. Make the most of your passion and imagination, but learn to adjust it to other Wardrobe Personalities when trying to win their business or friendship. A Creative is likely to be thinking about the next idea, while other personalities are still trying to digest the content of her previous comments!

Personal image tips:

- You may need to tone down your style, by wearing less colourful or flamboyant combinations if working in a conservative environment.
- If caring for the environment is important to you, you can show how you can re-invest or use old items and not necessarily always need new clothes.
- When others try to change you to be more conventional, particularly in your personal life, resist and be confident that you are creative.

Understand other Wardrobe Personalities:

- You should not feel uncomfortable with your appearance when you are with more conventional Wardrobe Personalities, but should appreciate them for having a conservative style.
- Don't be concerned by others' opinions, but show how your creative approach can benefit others as their approach might benefit you.
- Appreciate and learn from others who have a less artistic view and appreciate them for their style.

Team player:

- You generally love life and have a happy-go-lucky attitude, which can help others to relax.
- You enjoy other people's company.
- Your inventive ideas and enthusiasm can wear off on others.

• • • • •

"The only thing that separates us from the animals is our ability to accessorize."

OLYMPIA DUKAKIS

CHAPTER SIX

Guess the Wardrobe Personality!

Now you have read about and understood the differences between the 10 Warbrobe Personalities, here is a fun test for you to take. There may be more than one Wardrobe Personality in the items shown, but there will always be a dominant one. Have a look at the following illustrations and see if you can guess which Wardrobe Personalities would wear these accessories:

(Answers at the end of the chapter).

1.   Pretty peep toe T-bar gold shoes with handwork beads over them.

Which Wardrobe Personality would wear this shoe?

❑ Casual	❑ Sporty
❑ Gamine	❑ Classic
❑ Chic Classic	❑ Dramatic
❑ Romantic	❑ Fashion Fad
❑ Ingénue	❑ Creative

2. Plain black leather ballerina shoes with robe detail.

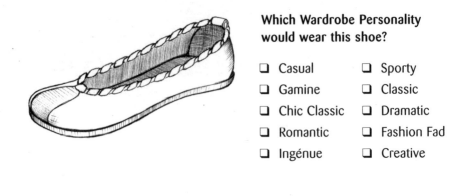

Which Wardrobe Personality would wear this shoe?

❑ Casual ❑ Sporty

❑ Gamine ❑ Classic

❑ Chic Classic ❑ Dramatic

❑ Romantic ❑ Fashion Fad

❑ Ingénue ❑ Creative

---

3. Elegant two-toned soft leather gloves in deep brown and camel.

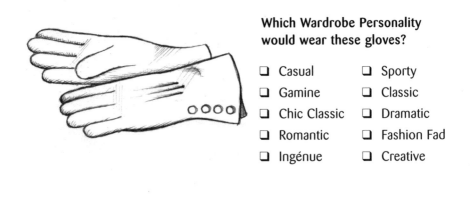

Which Wardrobe Personality would wear these gloves?

❑ Casual ❑ Sporty

❑ Gamine ❑ Classic

❑ Chic Classic ❑ Dramatic

❑ Romantic ❑ Fashion Fad

❑ Ingénue ❑ Creative

---

4. Trendy trilby hat from current collection as worn by celebrities.

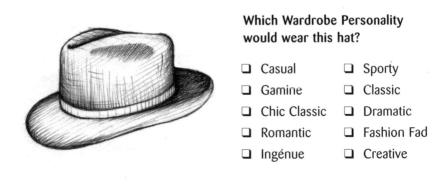

Which Wardrobe Personality would wear this hat?

❑ Casual ❑ Sporty

❑ Gamine ❑ Classic

❑ Chic Classic ❑ Dramatic

❑ Romantic ❑ Fashion Fad

❑ Ingénue ❑ Creative

5. Fashion-forward soft suede sheepskin boots.

Which Wardrobe Personality would wear these boots?

❑ Casual	❑ Sporty
❑ Gamine	❑ Classic
❑ Chic Classic	❑ Dramatic
❑ Romantic	❑ Fashion Fad
❑ Ingénue	❑ Creative

---

6. Unusual bold stripped platform sandals wrapped in fabric with a white buckle.

Which Wardrobe Personality would wear this shoe?

❑ Casual	❑ Sporty
❑ Gamine	❑ Classic
❑ Chic Classic	❑ Dramatic
❑ Romantic	❑ Fashion Fad
❑ Ingénue	❑ Creative

---

7. Brushed cotton baseball cap with velcro adjustable strap.

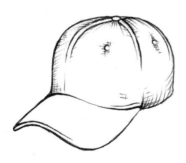

Which Wardrobe Personality would wear this hat?

❑ Casual	❑ Sporty
❑ Gamine	❑ Classic
❑ Chic Classic	❑ Dramatic
❑ Romantic	❑ Fashion Fad
❑ Ingénue	❑ Creative

8.   Red framed sunglasses with dark lenses and feminine diamante trim.

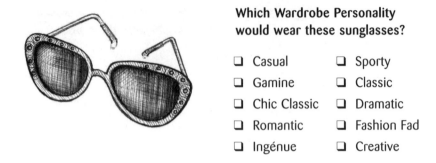

Which Wardrobe Personality
would wear these sunglasses?

❑ Casual	❑ Sporty
❑ Gamine	❑ Classic
❑ Chic Classic	❑ Dramatic
❑ Romantic	❑ Fashion Fad
❑ Ingénue	❑ Creative

9.   Oversized hoop earrings with glitter finish to sparkle in the light.

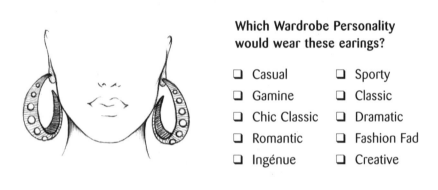

Which Wardrobe Personality
would wear these earings?

❑ Casual	❑ Sporty
❑ Gamine	❑ Classic
❑ Chic Classic	❑ Dramatic
❑ Romantic	❑ Fashion Fad
❑ Ingénue	❑ Creative

10.   Practical and fair-trade long plain wool scarf.

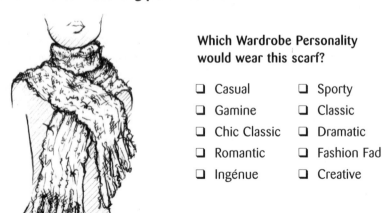

Which Wardrobe Personality
would wear this scarf?

❑ Casual	❑ Sporty
❑ Gamine	❑ Classic
❑ Chic Classic	❑ Dramatic
❑ Romantic	❑ Fashion Fad
❑ Ingénue	❑ Creative

11. Chic 18 carat gold ball earrings.

Which Wardrobe Personality would wear these earings?

- ❑ Casual
- ❑ Gamine
- ❑ Chic Classic
- ❑ Romantic
- ❑ Ingénue

- ❑ Sporty
- ❑ Classic
- ❑ Dramatic
- ❑ Fashion Fad
- ❑ Creative

---

12. Exceptional value lightweight glide-on texture and petal-shaped tip for precise application.

Which Wardrobe Personality would wear this lipstick?

- ❑ Casual
- ❑ Gamine
- ❑ Chic Classic
- ❑ Romantic
- ❑ Ingénue

- ❑ Sporty
- ❑ Classic
- ❑ Dramatic
- ❑ Fashion Fad
- ❑ Creative

Answers:

Wardrobe Personalities in brackets are Secondary Wardrobe Personalities.

1 = Ingénue (Romantic)	7 = Sporty
2 = Gamine	8 = Romantic (Fashion Fad)
3 = Chic Classic	9 = Dramatic
4 = Fashion Fad (Dramatic)	10 = Casual (Sporty)
5 = Fashion Fad (Casual)	11 = Chic Classic (Classic)
6 = Creative (Dramatic)	12 = Classic (Chic Classic)

• • • • •

"Dressing is a way of life."

YVES SAINT LAURENT

CHAPTER SEVEN

Our Secondary Personalities

Having completed the questionnaire you will probably have noticed that you are a mix of more than one Wardrobe Personality, with one more dominant and other secondary personalities. Your primary personality is often likely to be more prominent at work or as a mother, whereas the secondary personality is likely to be more evident in your personal or social life. The combination of the two will be reflected in the choice of items you like and purchase, with the secondary personality often coming to the fore in your accessories or what you prefer to wear when relaxing at home. Your secondary personality is very important, as it will help you to distinguish yourself from other people with the same primary Wardrobe Personality.

To help you understand the differences that may be evident from combinations of various Primary and Secondary personalities I offer some examples:

Casual/Creative

A fashion journalist, a Casual, will wear comfortable informal clothes and shoes and will often look untidy. Her second characteristic, Creative, will manifest itself in unusual combinations of styles or fabrics and textures, with several highly colourful or patterned items, e.g. colourful scarf, patterned tights, check tweed skirt, black velvet jacket and unusual items of jewellery and strong eye make –up when dressing up. As a Casual, her tendencies will be represented by casual style clothes, unstructured hair, unpolished shoes, loose-fitting clothes and little make-up (mascara). Overall, her wardrobe will be full of informal clothes in a variety of colour and textures and her hobbies are likely to include design, music (rock and roll or R&B), music festivals, theatre, art and reading.

Casual/Romantic

A nurse will wear uniform for work and will like comfortable flat shoes; she will like some make-up, e.g. lipstick, mascara and eye liner (Romantic) and her hairstyle is likely to have movement and may often change colour or have various highlights as she likes to look feminine (Romantic). In her personal life, she will always like to wear make-up, some jewellery (handcrafted or beads (Casual)). The Casual characteristics reflected in informal style clothes in natural fibres, especially denim skirts or jeans, wool jumpers and flat shoes although usually with detail and colour (Romantic). Being a Romantic she will dress up when socialising and enjoy mixing with male company. She will probably like cooking, modern music or dancing.

Fashion Fad/Gamine

A young woman works in a ladies clothes shop. As a Fashion Fad she will always be up-to-date with the latest trends. With her second characteristic – Gamine – she keeps a slim physique and always looks tidy in or out of work. Her hair will be in the latest style and he shoes will be from a fashionable brand, but usually flats for comfort, e.g. pumps or pixie boots. In her personal life she will dress casually in denim skirt or jeans with fashionable trainers and no make-up. She will enjoy buying clothes, will have a variety of accessories and will spend time getting ready to go out, ensuring every detail is right. She will regularly buy women's fashion magazines, watch music channels and reality TV programmes to follow the latest trends.

Sporty/Romantic with Dramatic tendencies

Unsurprisingly, a gym teacher, who swims, plays netball, has walking or cycling holidays is a Sporty. She will like to dress in comfortable jogging gear and, as a Dramatic, will like spending money on new gadgets such as a sports car, the latest mobile or trying new sports. Her Romantic characteristic will show through in wearing clothes in different colours, wearing a bold watch (Dramatic) and, possibly a bracelet and/or necklace (Romantic). She is likely to have her hair long to wear up when playing sports or short and spiky.

She will wear little make-up, possibly mascara and lip gloss for work, but colourful eyes and lips and nail varnish at weekends. Her wardrobe will be mostly casual in bold designs and strong colours, e.g. fashionable jeans, very high boots, chunky belt with a fashionable low cut fancy blouse. She will have lots of clothes and accessories (Romantic), top brand trainers, several boots and shoes with a selection of jewellery and make-up. Her grooming will be sharp and she will be confident (especially playing sport and meeting new people), probably quite loud, as she likes to be noticed (Dramatic). Her interests will be mostly sports as well as modern music, cooking and clothes shopping.

Chic Classic/Romantic

A businesswoman, is a Chic Classic with Romantic secondary characteristics. As a Chic Classic she is likely to dress in a classic way, but in a contemporary style (i.e. a jacket with trousers or skirt in a modern fabric or cut). The Romantic aspect of her Wardrobe Personality will be evident in a more overtly colourful jacket or top and a heeled crocodile-skin shoe. Her hair will be neat, but have some movement with some highlights. As a Romantic she will like to wear a variety of make-up and jewellery, which will be of good quality as a a Chic Classic. As a Romantic she will have a variety of handbags, shoes, make-up and accessories, which will all be well organised and kept in their place

(Chic Classic). She will be a good networker as she will be comfortable socialising in mixed company. Her hobbies are likely to include cuisine (food and wine), entertaining, music, creative and cultural pursuits.

Ingénue/Classic

A Personal Assistant, works for a senior manager in a retail clothes company and enjoys dancing as a hobby and singing with the local choral society. She likes to wear a brown jersey wrap dress with pink and beige flowers or an espresso-coloured skirt suit with floral satin jacquard trims and a sugar pink top with a lace trim. She wears brown high heels with a beige/pink rose on them, has several dainty pieces of jewellery, always has a full make-up on every day, with the lipstick quite heavy and in a soft pink shade. Her hair is long and neat (classic) but with lots of waves and movement (Ingénue). As an Ingénue she likes very feminine detail, she likes to help people and is very caring. The classic aspect is to wear formal clothes that look smart plus she is a good organiser, which ideally suits her role as a PA.

It is the combination of the Wardrobe Personalities that helps you to be unique, which will determine how you interpret what is appropriate for a function or event and help you decide what is suitable for business casual dress. It will affect the combination of styles and colours you like and buy, and the number and type of accessories you will go for, be they colourful, large, big or discreet. As you will have seen from the previous examples, it will affect which items you like to put together for your personal and business life, what hobbies and homewares you prefer and what combination of long term friends you are likely to have.

As you grow and develop so, perhaps, will the combination of your Wardrobe Personality. I hope that this book will help you to appreciate the differences and how better to show your inner you in the clothes and accessories you chose to wear.

You might find you leave a large firm and set up your own business whereupon you may become more casual, creative or dramatic and wish to adapt your style of clothes accordingly. I often find clients like to have a refresher consultation with me when their life changes, so that I can help them bring out characteristics they hadn't recognised they really had and more accurately show their new personal image.

• • • • •

"Just around the corner in every woman's mind - is a lovely dress, a wonderful suit, or entire costume which will make an enchanting new creature of her."

WILHELA CUSHMAN

CHAPTER EIGHT

Appreciating all Wardrobe Personalities

In Chapter 5, you will have discovered many of the differences between Wardrobe Personalities and how, through the combination of primary and secondary, they will influence a person's character. You may well have recognised Wardrobe Personalities of friends, members of your family or even of work colleagues.

This can help you to understand why sometimes:

- **You may not like what they wear.**
- **They behave in a different way to you.**
- **They may be less or, indeed, more organised than you.**
- **People are more fashionable, creative or casual than you.**

In recognising this, you are able to appreciate them for who they are, whilst also feeling entirely comfortable and confident in yourself. That is why you are most likely to get on better with friends with whom you have at least one Wardrobe Personality in common. When you find yourself in the company of others that may have completely contrary Wardrobe Personalities to you, then you will be able to adapt your behaviour, style and approach, as you consider necessary, to prevent any real clash of personalities!

How we interact with others at work, in our neighbourhood, at school or at social functions is very important. Although we will tend to be drawn to people who dress in similar styles to us and with whom we will feel more comfortable, it is good to mix with different Wardrobe Personalities and network with people to learn and understand different Wardrobe Personalities. It helps us to develop and learn more about other interests.

This book seeks to help you to recognise other people's Wardrobe Personalities and why they may not do things the way you do. It may even assist you better to understand your partner and to recognise why you sometimes differ in ideas; for example, how one of you may be more tidy (or untidy), fashionable, creative or practical than the other.

By recognising the Wardrobe Personalities of people you interact with, you should understand them better and learn to expect certain behaviour from them. You will now understand why you get on better with some people than others. In the work environment you may also understand why some colleagues are invariably late or struggle to meet deadlines and you can adapt your behaviour or plan accordingly. It is unlikely that they are going to change completely, although they can recognise the areas in which they need to improve and develop tighter habits or regimes.

You may learn that certain Wardrobe Personalities find change difficult and that they will need convincing as to why change is necessary. Others will be slower with their work, but more methodical, while some may be quick, but lack attention to detail. All these people have their own unique strengths and can work as a team to achieve an ideal result.

Tuning into the Wardrobe Personalities of others

If you are involved in recruiting staff you will also recognise the Wardrobe Personality traits of candidates and this will provide you with a valuable insight into people. Alternatively, if you apply for a role in a new organisation, you will be able to work out its Wardrobe Personality and present yourself accordingly. Of course, you will have to be happy that its culture matches your own Wardrobe Personality. When you present or deliver information to people, your understanding of their Wardrobe Personality will enable you to adapt your performance to suit them best (i.e. go into significant detail or stick to the big picture).

I recently noticed an accessories shop promoting an evening where people were offered a gift from another company. The only problem was that the two companies attracted different Wardrobe Personalities, so the evening was not as successful as it may have been. If the company had offered gifts from similar Wardrobe Personalities, customers would have been keener to attend the event and those attending would have talked more about their gifts and shown more appreciation. The event would have been much more memorable.

As we go through our daily lives we meet so many people with differing styles and behaviour. Understanding Wardrobe Personalities helps us all to communicate with all of them more successfully. Some people do not like too much detail, while others require a lot. Some people hate change while others are always looking for change or needing something new to keep them interested. Not all of us are imaginative and creative. We can be just as happy with something straightforward and simple. I am sure we all know some people who seem naturally neat and organised, while others have a more relaxed style, or appear to live in a state of perpetual chaos, always rushing around and never planning.

It may sound a little contrived, but you can tell all this from a person's appearance. If you are responsible for staff, being able to identify their Wardrobe Personalities will make it easier for you to recognise their strengths and to understand areas where they may not be so strong and then to be able to delegate work accordingly. You need to appreciate that you can never change people completely, but you can certainly organise them and their work more appropriately to get the best out of them.

The value of understanding our sense of style

From a personal perspective, I have found it invaluable to know about Wardrobe Personality when clients come to see me or when I meet professionals or tradesmen whom I might hire for a project. With clients, I will know by their appearance whether they will be interested in the latest trends and how much information they are likely to need (i.e. lots of detail or big picture). A Casual will want the big picture, particularly on style, while the Gamine will want much more information and will often question the reasons why something is what it is!

The Casual will need help to look smart yet relaxed, while the Classic needs help on how to dress down.

With professionals and tradesmen, I have used Wardrobe Personality to help me select an interior designer, a solicitor and a carpenter. I personally prefer a solicitor with Classic or Gamine in their personality to ensure they have covered the detail in legal documentation. However, a Casual may be more assertive and quicker if it is a rush job where detail is less important and will have a more casual approach to deal with. However, for an interior designer I would choose someone who relates to my own Wardrobe Personality and personal style, but has greater creativity to give me fresh ideas. Similarly with my hairdresser, a Creative or Romantic will encourage me to be less neat and formal on occasions and to have unusual or fashionable ideas to change my styles.

Wardrobe Personalities in the corporate world

It is also important to remember that companies or organisations have a culture, which can be imposed by the founder, directors or senior management. These decision-makers will wish to lead the company in a certain direction and generate a certain style (either entrepreneurial – Romantic/Creative, adventurous and go ahead – Sporty/Dramatic or highly organised with clear management structures and responsibilities – Classic/Chic Classic).

We can see this in everyday living, such as the style and delivery of news and current affairs on breakfast television. GMTV comes across as Romantic, Fashion Fad and Sporty, both in the subjects they emphasise and the way in which the programme is delivered. By contrast, the BBC appears mostly Classic, Gamine or Sporty, although some of the presenters, at times, do appear rather more Casual.

Recruitment and Human Resources – This is one of the areas where knowledge will be beneficial as it is clearly vitally important to recruit people that will bring not only the right skills, but also the right approach to an existing team. The wrong individual who may clash with or fail to complement an existing team could end up being disruptive and causing discontent. A person's appearance will give vital clues about who they are and their Wardrobe Personality.

When it comes to shopping to suit your Wardrobe Personality there is a huge variety of styles on offer that will appeal to different Wardrobe Personality types, e.g. Waitrose to Sainsbury's, Mercedes-Benz to BMW or Audi. Department Stores such as Liberty's will appeal to Fashion Fads, Creatives and Romantics, Harrods to Chic Classics and Dramatics, House of Fraser to Romantics and Classics, whereas John Lewis is regarded as more traditional, selling quality and reliability, and tending to attract Classics and Gamines.

Compare Virgin Atlantic with British Airways, or Starbucks with Costa Coffee, they all have a different style that may well attract certain Wardrobe Personalities.

Understanding the various Wardrobe Personalities can also benefit many businesses. For instance:

Hairdressers

Womens' Wardrobe Personality will determine their attitude to their hair in terms of style, cut and colouring. A Casual will not want to spend time on her hair and will prefer an easy wash and go style, whereas a Romantic will be prepared to spend more time and will want a cut that gives some movement and really makes them feel good. By recognising this, hairdressers can advise people accordingly and provide them with the type of service they will really appreciate. Also, they should consider employing a variety of Wardrobe Personalities amongst their stylists/staff to appeal to the various client groups.

Graphic designers and website designers

Understanding the Wardrobe Personality of a small business person will help the designer to develop a website or logo that more appropriately reflects their customer and is more in line with their own Wardrobe Personality, rather than coming forward with ideas that may be too creative or dramatic.

Small clothes retailers

Often the proprietor will choose clothing that she likes and which suits her own Wardrobe Personality; this will restrict their type of client. By understanding all the other Wardrobe Personalities, she can ensure that the stock comprises a broad range of products. As I hope you will have discovered, buying clothes that really match your Wardrobe Personality is vitally important and employing assistants who understand this and will help you choose what is right and what to avoid is invaluable. A truly satisfied customer will generally come back! Mary Portas, in the programme Mary, Queen of Shops has helped update small retail businesses and it is interesting to note that the proprietor has often naturally updated and adapted her (or his) own Wardrobe Personality at the same time.

Dating agencies

What a revelation it would be if people were selected for each other based on complementary Wardrobe Personalities. Dare I suggest that the success rates might be much higher?

We are all 'buying' other people at some level or other. You may well find that you will tend to attract clients of similar Wardrobe Personalities or at least with one Wardrobe Personality in common. This can be very helpful, particularly if you are a sole trader and this can be used for your marketing. So, it is worth finding out the Wardrobe Personality of the people with whom you work best, but not forgetting how to appreciate other Wardrobe Personalities and adapt how you use their services or work with them.

• • • • •

"What a strange power there is in clothing."

ISAAC BASHEVIS

CHAPTER NINE

Take Action!

Now that you have recognised your Wardrobe Personality what should you do to make it work for you and enhance your lifestyle? Really, you need to take some action straight away and get the process moving. It will take an initial time commitment, but you will be more than rewarded by the time, effort and money you will save in the future.

So, put some time aside to check out your wardrobe, even if you are a Casual and not interested in clothes, as a little time well spent now will pay dividends in the future. Having a wardrobe of clothes you enjoy will encourage you to take more interest in your appearance, which in turn will benefit you all round.

Step 1

Firstly and most importantly, take an hour or so to look at the clothes in your wardrobe. Check the feel of the fabrics and decide whether you like them or not. Are there clothes you never wear due to the fabric, the style or because you just don't feel good in them? To be sure, try the items on and experiment by pairing them with other items and/or accessories. Put those that you like and wear regularly in one pile, those you like, but wear infrequently in another, and those that you don't like or never wear in a third pile.

Step 2

Take those items that are in the third pile and store them somewhere else, in a case or even in a bin liner, and see if you actually miss them. You will probably find you don't.

This will have the double benefit of creating space for new clothes that really do suit you and ensuring that your decision-making about what to wear each day is easier. Also, much more tangibly, you should notice your spirits lift because you will know that you are wearing clothes that show you as you want to be seen. Feeling positive about yourself will increase both your confidence and performance.

Step 3

Organise your wardrobe and start planning what type of clothes you think you need to buy to suit your lifestyle. Make a list of what you need, including accessories to compliment what you already have and to more clearly show your Wardrobe Personality for both your work and your social life.

Step 4

Decide on a budget, prioritise what you need and then purchase the clothes and accessories on your list, bearing in mind what may be needed for the season ahead. (See the next chapter for suggestions of what brands to buy that suit your Wardrobe Personality.)

Step 5

Don't stop there! You must from time to time review your wardrobe and, whenever you need something new, ensure that what you buy is in tune with your Wardrobe Personality. For some, it will be more difficult than others, but do try to look at clothing or style magazines, or the internet, or visit shops occasionally to review what clothes are in stock, to plan additions to your wardrobe.

Adjustment at various stages in your life

You wardrobe may need amending as you mature and particularly when you go through the various life stages e.g. leaving home, first job, becoming a mother, entering the menopause and retirement. You may well find you prefer different styles and fabrics during some of these periods. For example, you may find, as a Romantic, when you are pregnant or going through the menopause, that you do not enjoy synthetic fibres, whereas you have in the past. You may, however, still prefer the softer fabrics and enjoy make-up, accessories and shoes; the styles or fabrics may just need adapting.

At my time of life, I have found that I prefer brushed cotton or softer cottons to fabrics with polyester, but I still like the softer feel. I also like to layer my clothes more, but I still want hairstyles, make-up, accessories and shoes to suit my Wardrobe Personality.

• • • • •

"Women usually love what they buy, yet hate two-thirds of what is in their closets."

MIGNON MCLAUGHLIN

CHAPTER TEN

Which Brands Suit Which Wardrobe Personalities?

Where to shop

Over the years, lifestyles have become more complex with so many options, more people travelling and an increasing pace of life. Nothing seems to stay the same for very long, including fashion and the types of styles that are appropriate to wear, so we need to understand how to adapt and change our styles of dress accordingly. It is vital that we know what we like and what suits our Wardrobe Personality for various events. We need to create the look that makes us feel confident and comfortable, and which appropriately displays our personal image. Once we understand that, we will be confident enough to adapt our clothes to suit our moods and circumstances. Sometimes, we need only make a few slight changes, such as accessories, hair or a simple item of clothing.

When I take a client shopping, the first thing I look at is her Wardrobe Personality, then her budget and then what is needed for the season. This helps me to decide the brands that will appeal whilst staying within budget. Then, when I help choose items I need to consider the fabrics in which she will feel comfortable and the styles that make her feel great. Obviously, I then need to consider body shape and the shades of colours that suit her best.

Be brave – try a new look

When she is trying on the clothes, I will discuss the fit, the look the clothes give (i.e. the style) and most importantly confirm that she is comfortable in the fabric and that she feels great. There are occasions when it may be a new look, so she might need persuading why it looks good. In this case, I always explain why I think it is good and how it fits in with her Wardrobe Personality. I never forget what her Wardrobe Personality is as I want her to not only look good, but to feel great every time she wears the clothes! She will not wear them if she is not happy in them and then it's a waste of money. The clothes must reflect who she is as a person; they must reflect her personal image and her personal brand and how she wants to come across. Above all, she must feel great as well as look great.

Here is a list of brands for you to consider to suit your Wardrobe Personality. Some brands you may feel are too expensive or not expensive enough, but I have tried to cover various price ranges so there should be something for everybody. They may also cover more than one Wardrobe Personality.

You need to be careful, however, as brands do occasionally change in style when a new designer or buyer is employed, as they will tend to reflect their own Wardrobe Personalities in what they do. Also, what I list below are only my suggestions, hopefully you will find others that reflect the "true you" and if you have any brands that you feel you would like added to the list or have any comments on these or others please do let me know – email **angela@appearancemanagment.co.uk.**

Casuals

Adidas, Asda George, Ben Sherman, Bhs, Boden, Calvin Klein, Crocs, Debenhams, Ecco, Fat Face, Gap, Gratton, Hush Puppies, Jasper Conran, Lacoste, Levi's, Littlewoods, Marks & Spencer, Matalan, Nicole Farhi, Peruvian, Primark, Reebok, Shoe Express, F&F Tesco, Warehouse.

Make-up for a Casual

Clinique, Mac, Marks & Spencer, Maybelline, No.17, Rimmel.

Sporty

Adidas, Asda George, Bench, Ben Sherman, Berghaus, Boss, Calvin Klein, Crew, Crocs, Diesel, DKNY, Dunlop, Ellie Gray, Emporio Armani, Fat Face, Firetrap, Fly London, French Connection, Fred Perry, Gap, Hawk, Henleys, Jasper Conran, Jigsaw, K Swiss trainer, Lacoste, Levi's, Lee Cooper, Lillywhites, Marks &

Spencer, Missoni, Nicole Farhi, Nike, North Face, Ocean Pacific, Paul Smith, Pepe Jeans, Peruvian, Pointer, Puma, Reebok – Air Max, Reiss, Sportshoe.com, Timberland, Uniqlo, Vans, Wrangler.

Make-up for a Sporty

Clinique, Jemma Khan, Mac, Marks & Spencer, Maybelline, Next, No.17, Prescriptive, Rimmel.

Gamine

Adidas, Armani, Ben Sherman, Bench, Berghaus, Betty Barclay, Boden, Calvin Klein, DKNY, Diesel, Emporio Armani, Energie jeans, Fat Face, Fred Perry, Gap, Gerard Darel, Hobbs, Jigsaw, John Lewis, Joseph, K Swiss trainer, Lacoste, M&S Autograph, M&S Limited Collection, Marc Jacobs, Marella, Miu Miu, Moschino, Next, North Face, Ocean Pacific, Olsen, Patsy Seddon, Paul Smith, Pepe Jeans, Peruvian, Phase 8, Poetry, Precis, Puma, Reebok – Air Max, Sahara, Sportshoe.com, Stella McCartney, Ted Baker, Timberland, Tods, Tommy Hilfiger, Ugg, Warehouse, Wrangler.

Make-up for a Gamine

Bobby Brown, Clinique, Mac, Marks & Spencer, Maybelline, No.17, Prescriptive.

Classics

Alex & Co., Aquascutum, Austin Reed, Ben Sherman, Betty Barclay, Bhs, Boden, CC, Clarks, Elvi, EWM, Fred Perry, French Connection, Gabor, Gerry Weber, Great Plains, House of Fraser, Jaeger, John Lewis, Jones Bootmaker, Lands End, Marks & Spencer, Marks & Spencer Autograph, Marella, Miu Miu, Next, Olsen, Poetry, Primark, Ted Baker, TieRack, Van Del, Viyella, Wallis, Weekenders.

Make-up a Classic

Clarins, Elizabeth Arden, Lancome, L'Oreal, No.7, Revlon.

Chic Classic

Armani, Bottega Veneta, Browns, Caroline Charles, Carvela, Catherine Walker, Chloe, Dior, Feraud, Gucci, Joyce Ridings, Harrods, Hermes, Kurt Keiger, Longchamp, Louis Vuitton, Marina Rinaldi, Max Mara, Miu Miu, Oscar de la

Renta, Patrick Cox, Paul Costello, Pringle of Scotland, Ralph Lauren, Salvatore Ferragamo, Selfridges, Wille, YSL.

Make-up for a Chic Classic

Chanel, Chantecaille, Dior, Elemis, Guerlain, Jo Malone, Kanebo, Space NK, Stila.

Dramatics

Alexander McQueen, Armani, Levi's, Browns, Burberry, Christian Dior, Dries Van Noten, Emporio Armani, Escada, Etro, Harvey Nichols, Jasper Conran, Julien Mcdonald, Jimmy Choo, Marc Jacobs, Miu Miu, Mulberry, NDC, Prada, Ralph Lauren, Roberto Cavalli, Selfridges, Tom Ford, Valentino, Versace, Vivienne Westwood,

Make-up for a Dramatic

Bare Essentials, Chanel, Crème de La Mer, Dior, Eve Lom, Jo Malone, Laura Mercier, Model Co. Nars, Tom Ford, VSL.

Romantics

Accessorize, Aldo, Antik Batik, Barratts, Bertie, Coast, Debenhams, Emporio Armani, Escada, Faith, Fenwicks, Gerard Darel, Ghost, Gina Bacconi, House of Fraser, Jacques Vert, James Lakeland, Jimmy Choo, Jigsaw, Karen Millen, L K Bennett, Lacoste, Liberty, Linea, Marks & Spencer Autograph, Marks & Spencer Collezioni, Miss Sixty, Nine West, Nougat, Office, Phase 8, Pied à Terre, Principles, Sass & Bide, Sticky Fingers, Ted Baker, Top Shop, Valentino, Versace, Whistles, Zandra Rhodes, Zara.

Make-up for a Romantic

Benefit, Bourjois, Elizabeth Arden, Espa, Estée Lauder, Max Factor, Rimmel, Shiseido, Virgin Vie, www.pout.co.uk.

Fashion Fad

7 for all mankind, Alexandra McQueen, Ash, Asos.com, Boss, Burberry, Citizens of Humanity, Converse, Crocs, D&G, Designers at Debenhams, Diesel, Ebay, Emporio Armani, Fenwicks, Firetrap, Fly London, H&M, Jamesjeans, Jasper Conran, Jimmy Choo, Levi's, Matalan, Morgan, Mulberry, New Look,

Office, Pepe Jeans, Pret à Porter, Pringle, Replay, Selfridges, Stella McCartney, TK Maxx, Top Shop Kate Moss, Yoji Yamamoto.

Make-up for a Fashion Fad

Aveda, Bliss, Jemma Khan, Mac, Model Co., Space NK, Versace.

Ingénue

Asos.com, Ben de Lisi, Dolce & Gabbana, Emporio Armani, Fenn Wright & Mason, Fenwicks, Ghost, Jasper Conran, Jigsaw, Kenzo, Miss Selfridge, Miss Sixty, Nougat, Miu Miu, Oasis, Phase 8, Ralph Lauren, Ted Baker, Top Shop, Valentino, Versace, Whistles.

Make-up for an Ingénue

Benefit, Bourjois, Elizabeth Arden, Espa, Estée Lauder, Max Factor, Virgin Vie, www.pout.co,uk.

Creative

Absolute vintage, All Saints, Asos.com, Beyond Retro, Bella Freud, Biba, charity shops, Christian Dior, Creative Recreation, D Squared, Ebay, J Lindberg, Karen Millen, Liberty, Oki-ni.com, Portobello Road Market, Primark, Replay, small unusual designer boutiques, Versace, Vintage, Vivienne Westwood, Yukka, Zandra Rhodes.

Make-up for a Creative

Benefit, Bourjois, Dior, Estée Lauder, Shu Uemura, Versace, YSL.

• • • • •

"You are never fully dressed until you wear a smile."

UNKNOWN

CHAPTER ELEVEN

Dressing to Suit Yourself

I hope my book will help you to develop your Wardrobe Personality, including bringing out your secondary Wardrobe Personality of which you may not have been aware. Most importantly, I hope that you will not only buy clothes to look and feel good in, but remember to buy to suit your Wardrobe Personality.

Disabled people

If you have a disability you rely more on some of your senses; by using those senses you can choose the clothes you wish to wear to suit your Wardrobe Personality. For example a blind person can bring out their Wardrobe Personality by ensuring they enjoy the feel of the fabrics and textures. Although you may not be able to see your hair you can feel whether you want it neat, short or flowing with movement. Your accessories can be large or small-scale, wooden, stone or metal. People in wheelchairs may want to emphasise their Wardrobe Personality more around their face and top half of their body, although if they love feminine shoes then colour or pattern in their shoes will be important too.

Children's Wardrobe Personality

If you have children I am sure you will notice how they can differ in approach, personality and the types and styles of clothing they prefer to wear. Even at an early age our Wardrobe Personality is developing and I would encourage you to recognise what it is and to let them create, obviously within reason, their own style with confidence (including creating habits for good grooming). I am convinced that this will enable them, with your guidance, to build on their own self-belief and help them to achieve what they really want in life.

Wardrobe Personality vs colouring and body shape

Although this book is about Wardrobe Personality, it is vitally important when buying clothes to consider body shape and colouring. Some people think body shape has an impact on Wardrobe Personality and that they go together. I have to confess that I do not agree. One of the reasons people think this is because some textures and fabrics are more suited to certain body shapes and sizes. However, there is such a variety and mixture of textures and fabrics today that you can learn to adapt your style even if some fabrics and textures do not initially suit your shape. You can also let your accessories, hairstyle and the colours you wear help to bring out your Wardrobe Personality. For instance, a petite curvaceous woman (with large bosoms, sloping shoulders and wide hips) may find it harder to dress as a Fashion Fad, than a tall, slim woman with a small bust and broad shoulders. However, she can wear a top, in a style to suit her, in the hottest colours of the season with stripes or patterns to suit her frame. Her hairstyle, shoes and accessories can all be up to the minute in the latest trends (again to suit her). There are always combinations that can be adapted to fit in with the latest season's looks and all body shapes.

Again, a person with a Gamine build may like to be a Dramatic/Romantic. She can achieve this by wearing accessories that are slightly larger relative to her smaller frame (e.g. earrings, buckle on belt, brooch rings, shoes) with a blouse in the strongest colours of her palette. A hairstyle that has some exaggeration in style and choosing a combination of fabrics will suit both Wardrobe Personalities. You may find you want to be a gamine in Wardrobe personality, but often put on weight and so are forever dieting. Recognise you do not have a gamine build and adapt your style; don't get fixated about keeping slim, as this may cause you to have slimming problems.

Remember, you are who you are and, although you may not be happy with your body shape, who is actually perfect? Would it be Kate Moss, Catherine Zeta Jones or Keira Knightley? The answer is 'all of these' or 'none of these'. Many people might prefer to be Dawn French, who may be shorter and plumper, but has a priceless sense of humour! Whatever you are, make the most of what you were born with, because none of us is perfect!

My wishes

Once you have finished reading the book I have four wishes for you:

1. That you start making the necessary changes to your wardrobe today. Try on clothes from your wardrobe and find out what are your favourites and why. Evaluate each style and discard those that you never wear and you now know are not your Wardrobe Personality; experiment by mixing and matching and adding accessories and make the clothes look different. Before the end of the day you will know a lot more about what to wear to make you feel good and look good and you will be on the road to knowing what to buy and what to avoid. Have fun with your wardrobe and make it part of your life. Remember – adjust your wardrobe throughout the rest of your life, as you change, grow and develop.

2. That you enjoy wearing the styles, fabrics and accessories to suit you and not what other people like.

3. That when you get dressed each morning you love the results and feel great – every day! On the odd occasion when you do not, you will know why and what to do about it. And remember, life isn't perfect.

4. Finally, when you look in the mirror and know that you look and feel great and are dressing to suit yourself, you will give yourself a big smile.

It's amazing what you can achieve when you feel and look good. Your self-esteem grows and your confidence blooms. Keep in mind how dressing to suit yourself will help you to look and feel fantastic.

I sincerely hope you have found my book both interesting and beneficial, and that you have learned something about your Wardrobe Personality. Keep the book for reference as you grow, change and develop.

I wish you all the best in the future.

Angela Marshall

Being Truly You - for Men
Discovering Your Own Unique Wardrobe Personality

Angela Marshall has also written a book for men. **Being Truly You for Men** will help you better understand the men in your life – be it personal or business. Find out about the different men's Wardrobe Personalities and where you can shop for, or with them. Maybe you would like to purchase a copy for a partner, friend, or relative?

To order **Being Truly You for Men** please contact:
Troubador Publishing Ltd, 9 De Montifort Mews,
Leicester LE1 7FW, UK
Tel: +44 (0)116 255 9311
e-mail: book@troubador.co.uk
www.troubador.co.uk

How would you like a private consultation with Angela Marshall?
Personal image consultations are available for individuals and groups, covering topics such as:
- Colour analysis
- Style consultation
- How to sort, organise and plan your wardrobe
- Personal shopping service
- Hint and tips on making the most out of networking
- Tips and reminders on business etiquette

To book an appointment call Angela on: +44 (0)1372 388 584
e-mail: angela@appearancemanagement.co.uk
www.appearancemanagement.co.uk